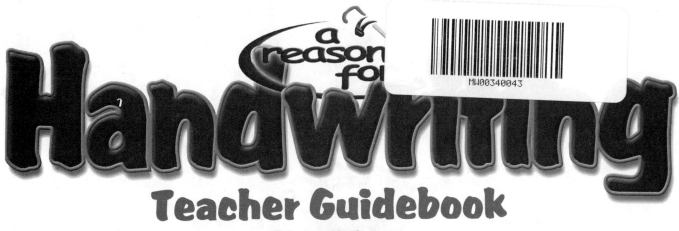

Handwriting

Teacher Guidebook

Transition

ISBN #0-936785-45-4

Published by Concerned Communications
700 East Granite • P.O. Box 1000 • Siloam Springs, AR 72761

Authors **Carol Ann Retzer, Eva Hoshino**
Publisher **Russ L. Potter, II**
Senior Editor **Bill Morelan**
Creative Director **Daniel Potter**
Copy Editor **Tricia Schnell Williams**
Proofreader **Trish Houston**
Illustrations **Rob Harrell**
Colorists **Josh & Aimee Ray**

Scripture translation selected for appropriate vocabulary level.
All verses are taken from *The Living Bible*, Tyndale House Publishers,
Wheaton, Illinois 60187. Used by permission.

printed on recycled paper

For more information about **A Reason For**® curricula,
write to the address above, call, or visit our website.

www.areasonfor.com
501.549.9000

A Personal Message from the Authors of

Handwriting

Dear Friends:

It seems like only yesterday. Recess had just ended, and as the children took out their pencils and paper, I began writing the day's handwriting lesson on the blackboard: "Only one cow, Clarabell, came."

Suddenly I stopped. How many hours had my students spent focusing on such meaningless sentences? Impulsively I erased the board, then wrote "Our God is so good!"

And from that humble beginning back in 1979, came **A Reason For® Handwriting**—the K-6 Scripture-based handwriting curriculum now used in thousands of private and parochial schools nationwide!

A Reason For® Handwriting was developed with three basic goals in mind. First, to help children develop proper handwriting skills. Second, to incorporate Scripture verses designed to inspire young hearts and minds. And third, to help children experience the fun and fulfillment of sharing God's Word with others.

In short, **A Reason For® Handwriting** helps integrate faith and learning to bring students closer to Christ. And after all, isn't that what our schools are all about?

May God richly bless as you continue to touch young lives for Him!

Carol Ann Retzer & Eva Hoshino
A Reason For® Handwriting

Table of Contents

Making the Transition
How to use this book

The Transition Student Workbook is designed to offer maximum flexibility in making the transition from manuscript to cursive handwriting. Extra manuscript lessons and extra cursive lessons allow you to begin the transition process at the time your school deems most appropriate.

Please note: No option uses ALL the pages in the Transition Student Workbook! Pages are perforated so teachers can easily remove unused lessons if desired before the school year begins. Extra pages can be discarded, or filed for later use in individual remediation.

OPTION 1: Transition at the start of the third 9 weeks of 2nd grade.

This is the recommended method and is used by most schools. It allows for 18 weeks of manuscript writing, 9 weeks of special transition practice, and 9 weeks of cursive practice. For most students, this timing correlates well with the development of small motor skills.

> **1st nine weeks:** use pages 21-38* **4th nine weeks:** use pages 125-142
> **2nd nine weeks:** use pages 39-56 Omit pages 57-74, 143-178
> **3rd nine weeks:** use pages 77-122
> *If extra manuscript review is needed, begin with the Practice Lessons on page 9 and omit pages 53-56.

Using this option, the correct curriculum sequencing would be:

1st grade - Manuscript A   4th grade - Cursive D
2nd grade - Transition   5th grade - Cursive E
3rd grade - Cursive C   6th grade - Cursive F

OPTION 2: Transition at the start of the fourth 9 weeks of 2nd grade.

This method is used by some schools. It allows for 27 weeks of manuscript writing, followed by 9 weeks of special transition practice. Its primary advantage is a little extra time for small motor skills development.

> **1st nine weeks:** use pages 21-38* **4th nine weeks:** use pages 77-122
> **2nd nine weeks:** use pages 39-56 Omit pages 125-178
> **3rd nine weeks:** use pages 57-74
> *If extra manuscript review is needed, begin with the Practice Lessons on page 9 and omit pages 53-56.

Using this option, the correct curriculum sequencing would be:

1st grade - Manuscript A   4th grade - Cursive D
2nd grade - Transition   5th grade - Cursive E
3rd grade - Cursive C   6th grade - Cursive F

OPTION 3: Transition to Cursive at the start of the 3rd grade.

This is the traditional method, very common 20 years ago, but currently losing popularity due to the continued push for acceleration. It allows the maximum time for small motor skills development. Students begin 3rd grade with 9 weeks of special transition practice, followed by 27 weeks of cursive writing.

1st nine weeks: use pages 77-122
2nd nine weeks: use pages 125-142
3rd nine weeks: use pages 143-160
4th nine weeks: use pages 161-178
Omit pages 7-74

Using this option, the correct curriculum sequencing would be:

1st grade - Manuscript A
2nd grade - Manuscript B
3rd grade - Transition
4th grade - Cursive D
5th grade - Cursive E
6th grade - Cursive F

OPTION 4: Transition to Cursive at the start of the 2nd grade.

This method is used by some schools with accelerated programs. Students begin 2nd grade with 9 weeks of special transition practice, followed by 27 weeks of cursive writing. Caution should be used with this approach due to readiness issues. Also, this method may not allow adequate time for students to completely master manuscript handwriting.

1st nine weeks: use pages 77-122
2nd nine weeks: use pages 125-142
3rd nine weeks: use pages 143-160
4th nine weeks: use pages 161-178
Omit pages 7-74

Using this option, the correct curriculum sequencing would be:

1st grade - Manuscript A
2nd grade - Transition
3rd grade - Cursive D
4th grade - Cursive E
5th grade - Cursive F
6th grade - No handwriting classes

Questions regarding the correct use of the Transition materials should be directed to:

Curriculum Director
Concerned Communications
P.O. Box 1000
Siloam Springs, AR 72761

Or for more immediate assistance, call toll-free: 800.447.4332

General Guidelines for
Teaching Handwriting

Handwriting is an essential skill for children and adults alike. Even in today's high-tech world, it's a skill we use every day!

Legible handwriting is a critical skill in the classroom, too. Students (even in high school and college) increasingly feel the need for quality handwriting as they face the essays required on many of today's standardized tests.

Unfortunately, there are no shortcuts in learning to write legibly. It does not occur automatically with age maturity, but is a learned motor skill that requires constant practice! And yet, "perfect" handwriting should never be an end in itself. Ultimately, the focus should be on the *message* rather than the process.

A Reason For® Handwriting provides the ideal message for your students to focus on — God's Word! In short, since success is achieved only by consistent, daily practice, why not focus that practice on the values found in Scripture verses?

Why Teach Manuscript?

It's much easier for children to imitate in writing what they see each day in reading. Manuscript is the style that dominates our world — from billboards, to street signs, to cereal boxes, to the textbooks students use. Thus manuscript writing is the logical starting point for beginning readers.

The Teacher's Role

Handwriting workbooks don't teach handwriting—TEACHERS do! Simply put, the process of learning legible handwriting is greatly enhanced by continued monitoring and guidance from an informed teacher.

Because children tend to imitate the teacher in their handwriting, you should become thoroughly familiar with all the letter forms used in *A Reason For*® Handwriting in order to demonstrate the individual letter strokes correctly. Even though it's similar to many traditional methods, *A Reason For*® Handwriting is a unique handwriting style. Please take a few moments to review the Manuscript Letter Formation Charts (see Appendix, page 152).

The Weekly Schedule

A Reason For® Handwriting should be part of your daily classroom schedule. Each section is designed to take 10 to 15 minutes to complete, since longer periods cause many children to tire and lose efficiency. Most students quickly grasp the simple weekly format, allowing them to focus their attention on the lesson tips, applications, and daily practice.

A great time to teach *A Reason For*® Handwriting is immediately after opening exercises. The program's Scripture-based content makes it ideal for beginning the day! And when you *begin* with handwriting, you can draw students' attention to practice letters throughout the school day.

Remember, it's counter-productive to let your students complete an entire week's lesson in one sitting! Only regular *daily* practice can bring effective results. The key is the *quality* of the practice, not the quantity!

Alternative Methods & Remediation

Many students are not visual learners, and need more than just a model to help them effectively improve their handwriting.

To maximize their learning experience, be sure to include some of the recommended alternatives (verbal description, board practice, Sky Writing, etc.) to demonstrate both letter size and formation. Board practice in small groups is especially helpful. It not only reinforces student learning, but also makes it easier to spot letter formation problems of individual students.

If students are having problems with specific letters, take time to review letter formation (see "letter formation charts," Appendix, page 152). It's really amazing how quickly a student's handwriting will improve when a specific problem area is remediated!

Evaluation & Motivation

Letting students know exactly what's expected is always helpful—especially when it comes to legible handwriting! As students are made aware of the evaluation system (see "Tips on Grading," page 9 and "Be a Five Star Student," Student Workbook, page 6), their work will improve remarkably. The evaluation system also provides a reference point to pinpoint specific areas (alignment, slant, size, shape, and spacing), and facilitates parent/teacher interaction. Scripture Border Sheets are also a powerful component of *A Reason For* ® Handwriting. When students know that their handwriting will be shared with others

(see "Ways to Share," page 10), they're motivated to do their *very best* work. You may assign specific border sheets each week, or let students select their own. (Note: Several border sheets feature holiday themes. Have students save these until the appropriate time.) Sharing Scripture Border Sheets can generate positive community interaction, and creates good will for your school!

Scripture Translation

Since *A Reason For* ® Handwriting was designed to teach elementary handwriting, using a Scripture translation with simple, easy-to-understand vocabulary was essential. Each Verse of the Week used in this series is taken from *The Living Bible* by Tyndale House Publishers.

Weekly
Lesson Format

The pattern of daily lessons in *A Reason For®* Handwriting repeats from week to week. This format minimizes the time needed each day for verbal instruction, and maximizes your students' time on task. Specific lesson tips, answers to discussion questions, and extended teaching suggestions for each lesson are found in the **Daily Lesson Plans** section, beginning on page 19.

Here is the suggested weekly lesson format:

Day One

Read the Verse of the Week together. Discuss the daily lesson tip. Point out the focus letters or words for the day.

Day Two

Read the Verse of the Week together. Review the focus letters or words for the day. Use the extended teaching tips as time permits.

Day Three

Same as Day 2.

Day Four

Read the Verse of the Week together. Have students practice the entire verse once or twice on a sheet of paper. Ask the students to select a Scripture Border Sheet from the back of their workbooks and begin decorating it.

Day Five

Challenge students to repeat the Verse of the Week from memory. Have students carefully write the Verse of the Week on their chosen Scripture Border Sheet, then finish decorating it. Discuss ways students can share their finished Scripture verses. (See page 10 for ideas.)

Tips on Grading

Grading System

There are five basic areas the teacher should consider when evaluating handwriting form. They are alignment, slant, size, shape, and spacing. The "Be a Five Star Student" section in the Student Workbook (page 6) has detailed descriptions of each area, and is designed to help you reinforce the evaluation process. Allowing 2 points for each item results in an easy-to-understand 10-point grading scale (see Appendix, page 175). If this system is used regularly, it helps students and parents understand how the final grade will be determined.

General Guidelines

It is important to keep handwriting evaluation as positive as possible. Look for the students' *best* work! Also, emphasize consistent writing from day to day, and focus on the *quality* of the student's handwriting rather than just quantity.

Student Folders

It's a good idea to keep a folder for each student with samples of his/her work. This should include pages from the beginning and ending of each grading period (either the alphabet or Day 4 practice). Thus, when grading time arrives, evaluation can be based on each individual student's progress.

Evaluation Sentence

The practice sentence at the bottom of the page (see also Student Workbook, page 6) contains all the letters of the alphabet. Ask students to write this sentence at the beginning of the grading period — then again at the end. Comparing the two will help you pinpoint specific letter problems.

This sentence may also be used for one-minute timed writings. While speed is not the primary concern in handwriting, some students may benefit from this practice. Be sure to encourage readability as well as speed!

The following practice sentence contains all the letters of the alphabet:

God created the zebras and foxes to walk, jump, and hide very quickly.

Ways to Share

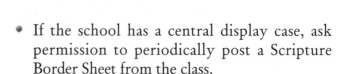

An exciting part of *A Reason For* **Handwriting** is the opportunity students have for sharing God's Word with others. While students enjoy writing and decorating the Verse of the Week, the real excitement begins when they *share* the finished Scripture Border Sheet with others.

- Place the verse in a spot where members of the family will see it every day.

- Make a placemat! Center the sheet on construction paper or a plain paper placemat. Laminate or cover with clear contact paper.

- Find someone who is housebound. Deliver the verse in person, and stay to visit.

- Give the decorated verse to grandparents. Don't forget a personal note — either on the back, or on a page of practice paper.

- Share the verse with someone who works at school: the secretary, custodian, principal, or even board members!

- Encourage other Christians. The church secretary can often provide names of those who'd appreciate a Scripture verse of encouragement.

- Take a trip to a nursing home. Have a pair of students visit each resident, then leave their verses to decorate the room.

- Give the verse to someone who is sick. Some hospitals will cooperate by placing the verses on patients' breakfast trays.

- Create an attractive bulletin board using the Scripture Border Sheets. Or select a special one each week, and display it in a special place in your classroom.

- If the school has a central display case, ask permission to periodically post a Scripture Border Sheet from the class.

- Check to see if your church would like to display the best verses, or enclose one with each copy of the church newsletter.

- Ask for a church mailing list. Send each family a Scripture Border Sheet and a personal note. Do a few each week. Students will be delighted with the positive response this will generate!

Suggested Cover Letter

People receiving the verses are often more responsive when a letter that describes the sharing program is included. Writing this letter on your school letterhead adds a nice touch. Here's a sample you can use:

Dear Friend,

Each week our class writes a Scripture verse as part of our handwriting lesson. This week we want to share a verse with you.

We hope you have a good week with God's blessing. We will be praying for you.

Sincerely,
(Your name)

Proper Positioning

Body Position

A good writing position provides comfort and balance. Encourage the students to:

- Sit comfortably back in the seat, facing the desk squarely.

- Place both feet flat on the floor.

- Lean slightly forward, but without letting the body touch the edge of the desk.

- Rest both forearms on the desk.

- Hold the paper in place with the free hand.

Paper Position

Right- and left-handed students should learn the same principle of paper placement. Students should place their paper at the same angle as the arm they use for writing (see illustrations). Demonstrate how the page can easily be moved up as the writing nears the bottom of the page. (Note: These paper positioning principles apply to both cursive and manuscript writing.)

Special attention should be given to left-handed students. Correct paper placement (see above) and pencil position will help the student write without a "hooked hand" position, or an exaggerated head tilt.

Pencil Position

The student should hold the pencil between the thumb and index finger, letting it rest lightly on the middle finger. The thumb should be about half an inch above the sharpened part of the pencil.

Please
Read This
First!

After the summer break, students often benefit from a focused review. The following **Practice Lessons** provide a quick, efficient method for reviewing manuscript letter formation.

These lessons are designed for one page each day, for a total of 10 days.

 **(see Student Workbook, page 9)**

LESSON FOCUS: Alphabet practice

DIRECTIONS: Have students write the entire alphabet — capital and lowercase. Start dots are provided to make this self-directed activity easier.

TEACHING TIP: Be sure to review the proper way to hold the pencil, as well as the correct posture and paper position (page 11), *before* students start this first lesson. While it's difficult to change the way a student holds a pencil, it's not impossible. Correcting problems now can impact a student's writing for the rest of his/her life. Positive praise can help make these changes permanent.

 **(see Student Workbook, page 10)**

LESSON FOCUS: Circle letter practice (c, o, a, d, e)

DIRECTIONS: Have students finish each line with the appropriate circle letter. Again, start dots are provided to make this self-directed activity easier.

TEACHING TIP: Most circle letters begin at the 2 o'clock position and go up and around to the left. The exception is the letter e. The e begins in the middle of the space and then goes up and around to the left. Have students look for the c as part of the e.

EXTENDED TEACHING: Challenge students to make words from the letters in this lesson: (dad, cod, deed, do, etc.). Also, don't forget that Sky Writing (see page 154) can be very helpful in reinforcing letter formation.

 **(see Student Workbook, page 11)**

LESSON FOCUS: Tall letter practice (l, h, b, t, k)

DIRECTIONS: Have students finish each line with the appropriate tall letter, using start dots.

TEACHING TIP: Most tall letters begin with a downstroke. The first stroke begins at the roofline and goes straight down to the floor. Other tall letters include the d and f. However, the d begins like the circle letters; the f begins just below the line and curves up and around before the downstroke.

EXTENDED TEACHING: Write the Lesson 3 letters (l, h, b, t, k) and the Lesson 2 letters (c, o, a, d, e) on the board. Challenge students to make words using these letters (hall, tall, ball, hat, bat, cat, talk, boat, lad, etc.) along with the vowels from Lesson 2. Remember that verbal descriptions of each letter can help lock the letter form in the mind of the student.

 (see Student Workbook, page 12)

LESSON FOCUS: Two-stroke letters (t, f, k, j, i)

DIRECTIONS: Have students finish each line with the appropriate two-stroke letter.

TEACHING TIP: Although the majority of manuscript letters may be written without picking up the pencil, the letters in this lesson require a second stroke. Sky Write and verbally describe these letters to imprint them in students' minds. These letters can also be written in rhythm to a one-two count. For example: The t is down/across, or one/two. Several students can write these letters on the board in rhythm as other students clap in time and chant: "one, two, one, two. . ."

EXTENDED TEACHING: Ask students what letters are tall letters *and* two-stroke letters? (t, f, k) Ask what two-stroke letters are missing from this list? (x, y) Remind students that letters may belong to more than one group. For example, the x and y are also slant stroke letters. To further extend this lesson, write the Lesson 4 letters (t, f, k, j, i) on the board along with the letters from lessons 2 and 3 (c, o, a, d, e, l, h, b, t, h). Challenge students to write words using only these letters: (doll, foot, jet, jello, coat, boat, let, cab, etc.).

 (see Student Workbook, Page 13)

LESSON FOCUS: Slantstroke letters (v, w, x, y, z)

DIRECTIONS: Have students finish each line with the appropriate slant stroke letter.

TEACHING TIP: Challenge students to see the v in other letters. The obvious ones are w and y — however, the v is also in the x and k if you look sideways! Point out that two of this lesson's letters (x and y) are made with two strokes. The other slantstroke letters are made without picking up the pencil (v, w, z). Challenge students to identify another letter that contains slant lines (k).

EXTENDED TEACHING: Students often enjoy making letters with pipe cleaners, clay, or cookie dough. You may even wish to bake the finished dough letters so students can eat them!

 **Lesson 6** (see Student Workbook, page 14)

LESSON FOCUS: Curve letters (r, n, m, s, u)

DIRECTIONS: Have students finish each line with the appropriate curve letter.

TEACHING TIP: While some curve letters begin with a downstroke, they also curve around. Challenge students to find other letters that begin like the letter r (n and m). Help them visualize the r as a part of an h. Use a cut-out letter n to help students discover a u when you turn it around and upside down. Identifying such similarities and differences will help strengthen the students' mental picture of these letters.

EXTENDED TEACHING: Challenge students to describe the letter s. Explore ideas such as calling it a "double curve" letter. . . or using s words such as slither, slide and slink in the description. (Example: The letter s begins just below the dotted line, curves up and slinks around in the middle, and then slithers back around.) Students will also enjoy making the letter s from a pipe cleaner. Also, challenge students to make a list of words that use curve letters (r, n, m, s, u, h) and circle letters (a, c, d, e, g, q). Possible answers include: ran, sun, man, mom, etc.

 **Lesson 7** (see Student Workbook, page 15)

LESSON FOCUS: Tail letters (p, q, y, g, j)

DIRECTIONS: Have students finish each line with the appropriate tail letter.

TEACHING TIP: Ask students to imagine sitting in a chair that's too tall. Remind them how tired their legs get when they can't reach the ground. Now, point out that tail letters want to touch the ground, too! Challenge them to write all the tail letters carefully so that the tails touch the ground.

EXTENDED TEACHING: Using a cut-out letter p, encourage students to discover other letters by changing it around. (Flipped up, it becomes a b. Turned over, it's a q with no tail. Flipped up from a q, it becomes a d.)

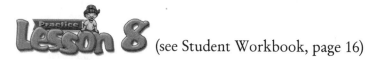 **Lesson 8** (see Student Workbook, page 16)

LESSON FOCUS: Capital letters (C, O, G, Q, P, R, B, D)

DIRECTIONS: Have students finish each line with the appropriate capital letter.

TEACHING TIP: Remind students to use start dots and arrow direction to have the best letter practice. Also, read aloud the two sentences that students can write after they have practiced the capital letters. Point out the exclamation point at the end of each sentence. Remind students that both sentences are something to be excited about!

EXTENDED TEACHING: These capital letters are grouped according to similar strokes. Challenge students to discover groupings. The first four letters are circle capitals; the last four are forward oval capitals. Also, some of these capitals are written with one stroke (C, O, G); others require two strokes (Q, P, R, B, D).

 (see Student Workbook, page 17)

LESSON FOCUS: Capital letters (A, X, M, N, K, V, W, Y, Z)

DIRECTIONS: Have students finish each line with the appropriate capital letter.

TEACHING TIP: For the most effective practice, these slant line capitals are grouped in similar stroke letter groups. Remind students to follow the arrows, and use the start dots to begin each letter.

EXTENDED TEACHING: All of these capital letters contain slant lines as part of the letter. Challenge students to identify which letters also contain straight lines (A, K, M, N, Y, Z).

 (see Student Workbook, page 18)

LESSON FOCUS: Capital letters (I, L, T, F, E, H, J, U, S)

DIRECTIONS: Have students finish each line with the appropriate capital letter.

TEACHING TIP: For the most effective practice, these downstroke and curve capitals are grouped in similar stroke letter groups. Remind students to follow the arrows, and use the start dots to begin each letter.

EXTENDED TEACHING: Have students identify the downstroke capitals from this lesson (I, L, T, F, E, H) and also capitals with some or all curve strokes (J, U, S). Challenge students to find four three-stroke capitals in this lesson (I, F, E, H). Ask students what other capital is also a three-stroke letter (A).

Please
Read This
First!

Before you begin the daily lessons, please make certain your students clearly understand the following:

> The mechanics of handwriting (see **Proper Positioning**, page 11).
> The format of the class (see **Weekly Lesson Format**, page 8).
> The evaluation process (see **Tips on Grading**, page 9).

It's also very important to have each student write the alphabet (capital and lowercase letters) on a sheet of paper, then sign his or her name and date it. You'll use this sheet later to pinpoint areas of special need, either for individual students, or for the entire class. It's also a good plan to keep this sheet on file to aid in evaluation for the next grading period.

Most importantly, remember that as you acknowledge and reward progress, the learning process is greatly enhanced!

Scripture Verse

"Love the Lord your God with all your heart, soul, and mind." Matthew 22:37

Tip of the Week

Manuscript handwriting is a skill you will use the rest of your life. This year, we'll be sharing ways to make your handwriting even better!

Letter Focus

A a, D d

NOTE:
Directions must be used as part of the Weekly Lesson Format. See page 6.

Lesson 1

TIP OF THE WEEK
Manuscript handwriting is a skill you will use for the rest of your life. This year, we'll be sharing ways to make your handwriting even better!

Day One   Practice the following letters and words from this week's Scripture.

A a

D d

and

Day Two   Continue practicing letters and words from this week's Scripture.

all

heart

21

Extended Teaching

• As you begin the weekly lessons, review the **Five Star** evaluation goals with your students (Student Workbook, page 6).

• Remind students that the books written by Matthew, Mark, Luke, and John are often referred to as the "Gospels."

For Discussion

Encourage students to think of ways they can show God they love Him. Ask them how this affects the way they treat others.

Day Three Continue practicing letters and words from this week's Scripture.

Lord

God

mind

Day Four Write this week's Scripture verse on a sheet of practice paper.

Love the Lord your God with all your heart, soul, and mind. Matthew 22:37

22

Scripture Verse

"Your care for others is the measure of your greatness." Luke 9:48

Tip of the Week

The letter o forms one part of the letter g — can you see it? Write both of these letters in one stroke, without picking up your pencil.

Letter Focus

Gg, Oo

NOTE:
Directions must be used as part of the Weekly Lesson Format. See page 6.

Lesson 2

Tip of the Week
The letter **o** forms one part of the letter **g** — can you see it? Write both of these letters in one stroke, without picking up your pencil.

Day One Practice the following letters and words from this week's Scripture.

Gg

Oo

go

Day Two Continue practicing letters and words from this week's Scripture.

greatness

for

23

✏ Extended Teaching

• Remind students that both the g and the o begin just below the center line and are written with a counter-clockwise circle without picking up the pencil.

• When a student is having difficulty with a letter it's helpful to practice the similar letter group (see page 161). Similar circle letters are o, a, d, g, and q.

✏ For Discussion

Discuss the concept of "random acts of kindness." Encourage students to watch for such opportunities at school this week. Remind them: "Your kind act is a secret! Don't let anyone know!"

Day Three Continue practicing letters and words from this week's Scripture.

care care

of of

measure measure

Day Four Write this week's Scripture verse on a sheet of practice paper.

Your care for others is the
measure of your greatness.
Luke 9:48

24

Lesson 3

Scripture Verse

"Come to terms quickly before it is too late."
Matthew 5:25

Tip of the Week

Your name is important — just like you! Write your letters carefully. Make certain they are the correct size and sit firmly on the line.

Letter Focus

Qq, Uu

NOTE:
Directions must be used as part of the Weekly Lesson Format. See page 6.

Lesson 3

TIP OF THE WEEK
Your name is important — just like you!
Write your letters carefully. Make certain
they are the correct size and sit firmly on the line.

Day One Practice the following letters and words from this week's Scripture.

Qq

Uu

quickly

Day Two Continue practicing letters and words from this week's Scripture.

Come

terms

25

Extended Teaching

• Students will benefit from extra practice of the g and q. Remind them to watch the direction of the tail!

• Visual and tactile learners will benefit from making these letters from pipe cleaners or clay.

For Discussion

Talk about the phrase "come to terms" with students. Challenge them to come up with helpful ways to settle an argument. Discuss these and look for specific applications.

Day Three   Continue practicing letters and words from this week's Scripture.

before before

late late

too too

Day Four   Write this week's Scripture verse on a sheet of practice paper.

Come to terms quickly
before it is too late.
Matthew 5:25

26

Scripture Verse

"Live in peace with each other." Mark 9:50

Tip of the Week

How are the lowercase c and e alike? How are they different? As you write these letters, make sure that they fill the entire space.

Letter Focus

Cc, Ee

NOTE:
Directions must be used as part of the Weekly Lesson Format. See page 6.

Lesson 4

TIP OF THE WEEK
How are the lowercase **c** and **e** alike?
How are they different? As you write these
letters, make sure that they fill the entire space.

Day One Practice the following letters and words from this week's Scripture.

Cc C

Ee E

each each

Day Two Continue practicing letters and words from this week's Scripture.

peace peace

Live Live

27

Extended Teaching

• Explore letter relationship by pointing out that the c is part of the e. Remind students that the beginning stroke of the e starts in the middle of the meeting room (see page 156).

• Ask the students how this Scripture verse relates to the last week's verse. (One deals with the problem, the other one suggests the goal or solution.)

For Discussion

Ask students, "Is it always easy to live in peace?" Explore ways to make your classroom more peaceful and less argumentative.

Day Three Continue practicing letters and words from this week's Scripture.

other other

in in

with with

Day Four Write this week's Scripture verse on a sheet of practice paper.

Live in peace with each other. Mark 9:50

26

🖉 Scripture Verse

"Be prepared, for you don't know what day your Lord is coming." Matthew 24:42

🖉 Tip of the Week

How are the lowercase b and p different? How are they alike? Be sure the tail of the p goes all the way to the ground.

🖉 Letter Focus

Bb, Pp

NOTE:
Directions must be used as part of the Weekly Lesson Format. See page 6.

Lesson 5

TIP OF THE WEEK
How are the lowercase b and p different? How are they alike? Be sure the tail of the p goes all the way to the ground.

Day One Practice the following letters and words from this week's Scripture.

Bb Bb

Pp Pp

prepare prepare

Day Two Continue practicing letters and words from this week's Scripture.

coming coming

Be Be

29

✏ Extended Teaching

• As the students practice the b and p, it's important that they make the letters with one stroke, beginning with the downstroke. Have students describe these letters aloud as they Sky Write. This will help them picture the letters in their minds.

• Remind students the b should touch the roofline, and the p should touch the ground.

✏ For Discussion

Discuss the importance of being prepared. Ask students, "What are some other areas of our lives where being prepared is very important?" (taking tests, receiving visitors, practicing home fire drills, etc.)

Day Three Continue practicing letters and words from this week's Scripture.

don't   don't

prepared   prepared

know   know

Day Four Write this week's Scripture verse on a sheet of practice paper.

Be prepared, for you don't know what day your Lord is coming. Matthew 24:42

30

Lesson 6

Scripture Verse

"Your strong love for each other will prove to the world that you are my disciples." John 13:35

Tip of the Week

Are your letters and words sitting firmly on the line? Think of your letters as birds sitting on a wire. Don't let them fall off!

Letter Focus

Ll, Vv

NOTE:
Directions must be used as part of the Weekly Lesson Format. See page 6.

Lesson 6

TIP OF THE WEEK
Are your letters and words sitting firmly on the line? Think of your letters as birds sitting on a wire. Don't let them fall off!

Day One Practice the following letters and words from this week's Scripture.

Ll

Vv

love

Day Two Continue practicing letters and words from this week's Scripture.

prove

will

31

Extended Teaching

• Help students focus on making sure their letters touch the line. Also, have them check alignment. Positive encouragement will help students do their best.

• As they practice the focus letter v, remind students of other slantstroke letters (k, w, x, y, and z). See page 161.

For Discussion

Ask students, "What are some ways that we can show we care for each other?" Have them make a list of nice things they could do for a friend. Now, challenge them to apply this attitude to everyone in their class.

Day Three Continue practicing letters and words from this week's Scripture.

strong

disciples

world

Day Four Write this week's Scripture verse on a sheet of practice paper.

Your strong love for each other will prove to the world that you are my disciples. John 13:35

32

✏ Scripture Verse

"Go home to your friends, and tell them what wonderful things God has done for you."
Mark 5:19

✏ Tip of the Week

Who was Mark, and why will you be writing his name this week? Other names this year are Matthew, Luke and John. Who were they? (They were disciples of Jesus, and the writers of the Gospels.)

✏ Letter Focus

Mm, Nn

NOTE:
Directions must be used as part of the Weekly Lesson Format. See page 6.

Lesson 7

TIP OF THE WEEK
Who was Mark, and why will you be writing his name this week? Other names this year are Matthew, Luke, and John. Who were they?

Day One   Practice the following letters and words from this week's Scripture.

Mm   Mm

Nn   Nn

done   done

Day Two   Continue practicing letters and words from this week's Scripture.

things   things

them   them

33

Extended Teaching

• Ask students to practice the curve letters h, n, m, and r. Have them Sky Write these letters, describing them aloud as they write them.

• Have one student verbally describe the lowercase h while another student attempts to write it on the board following their directions. Change students and do it again using the n, m, and r.

For Discussion

Have students make a list of good things God has blessed them with. Now have them take turns sharing their lists with each other in groups of three.

Day Three Continue practicing letters and words from this week's Scripture.

Mark   Mark

wonderful   wonderful

home   home

Day Four Write this week's Scripture verse on a sheet of practice paper.

Go home to your friends,
and tell them what wonderful
things God has done for you.
Mark 5:19

34

Lesson 8

✏ Scripture Verse

"If you are filled with light within, then your face will be radiant too." Luke 11:36

✏ Tip of the Week

Think how you have to stretch to reach the top shelf. This week, help your tall letters (d, f, h, l and t) stretch all the way to the top line.

✏ Letter Focus

F f, H h

NOTE:
Directions must be used as part of the Weekly Lesson Format. See page 6.

TIP OF THE WEEK

Think of how you have to stretch to reach the top shelf. This week, help your tall letters (d, f, h, l, and t) stretch all the way to the top line.

Lesson 8

Day One Practice the following letters and words from this week's Scripture.

F f

H h

filled

Day Two Continue practicing letters and words from this week's Scripture.

light

within

35

Extended Teaching

• Point out the two-stroke tall letters in this Scripture verse (f, k and t). The downstroke is written first. Ask students to find the "k" in this verse. (See "Luke" in the text reference.)

• Even though d is a tall letter, the circle part is written first.

For Discussion

Ask students to come up with ways they can be "filled with light." Talk about the relationship between our "inside" and our "outside."

Day Three Continue practicing letters and words from this week's Scripture.

face _face_

then _then_

radiant _radiant_

Day Four Write this week's Scripture verse on a sheet of practice paper.

If you are filled with light within, then your face will be radiant too. Luke 11:36

36

Lesson 9

Scripture Verse

"Oh, how I praise the Lord. How I rejoice in God my Savior!" Luke 1:46,47

Tip of the Week

Two lowercase letters that are almost look-alikes are i and j. Remember, the j has a tail just like a monkey. Don't forget to dot both letters.

Letter Focus

Ii, Jj

NOTE:
Directions must be used as part of the Weekly Lesson Format. See page 6.

Lesson 9

TIP OF THE WEEK

Two lowercase letters that are almost look-alikes are i and j. Remember, the j has a tail just like a monkey. Don't forget to dot both letters.

Day One Practice the following letters and words from this week's Scripture.

Ii

Jj

rejoice

Day Two Continue practicing letters and words from this week's Scripture.

praise

how

37

Extended Teaching

• Remind students that the i and j are written with a downstroke, and that the dot is added after the letter is written. Make certain students use a dot — not a small circle or dash.

• Point out the size difference between the i and j. Verbally describe the letters as students practice them (page 162).

For Discussion

Have students make a list of things that make them joyful — things for which they "praise the Lord." Then ask students to share their lists with each other.

Day Three Continue practicing letters and words from this week's Scripture.

Savior Savior

my my

Oh Oh

Day Four Write this week's Scripture verse on a sheet of practice paper.

Oh, how I praise the Lord.
How I rejoice in God my
Savior! ♫ Luke 1:46, 47

38

Lesson 10

✏ Scripture Verse

"Love your neighbor as much as you love yourself." Matthew 22:39

✏ Tip of the Week

The lowercase y is one of the two-stroke letters. How many other two-stroke letters can you find in this week's verse?

✏ Letter Focus

Uu, Yy

NOTE:
Directions must be used as part of the Weekly Lesson Format. See page 6.

Lesson 10

TIP OF THE WEEK
The lowercase y is one of the two-stroke letters. How many other two-stroke letters can you find in this week's verse?

Day One   Practice the following letters and words from this week's Scripture.

Uu   Uu

Yy   Yy

you   you

Day Two   Continue practicing letters and words from this week's Scripture.

your   your

much   much

39

Extended Teaching

• Point out the two-stroke letters found in this verse (i, f and t).

• Remind students that the capital letter Y is written like a v with a stem, and that both the capital and lowercase y's are two-stroke letters.

• Make a point to commend students who are using correct posture and paper position.

For Discussion

In this verse, Jesus gives a fundamental guideline about how we should treat others. Divide your students into small groups to discuss the meaning of this verse, then have them share their thoughts with the class.

Day Three Continue practicing letters and words from this week's Scripture.

yourself

neighbor

as

Day Four Write this week's Scripture verse on a sheet of practice paper.

Love your neighbor as much as you love yourself. Matthew 22:39

40

Scripture Verse

"Though all heaven and earth shall pass away, yet My words remain forever true." Luke 21:33

Tip of the Week

The capital R begins with a straight downstroke. The capital W is written with all slanting lines. Sit straight like the R as you write your words this week.

Letter Focus

Rr, Ww

NOTE:
Directions must be used as part of the Weekly Lesson Format. See page 6.

Lesson 11

TIP OF THE WEEK
The capital R begins with a straight downstroke. The capital W is written with all slanting lines. Sit straight like the R as you write your words this week.

Day One Practice the following letters and words from this week's Scripture.

Rr

Ww

words

Day Two Continue practicing letters and words from this week's Scripture.

away

remain

41

Extended Teaching

• Encourage students to practice slantstroke letters k, w, v, x, y, and z. Show students that two letters (k and z) are a combination of slant and straight.

• Describe differences in making the w and v versus the x and y. (The w and v are written without picking up the pencil; the x and y are two-stroke letters.)

For Discussion

In view of this week's Scripture verse, discuss what things are always the same, and what things change in life. (Same: Basic principles found in Scripture, Jesus, God, etc. Change: seasons, food preferences, where we live, etc.)

Day Three Continue practicing letters and words from this week's Scripture.

earth   earth

true   true

forever   forever

Day Four Write this week's Scripture verse on a sheet of practice paper.

Though all heaven and earth shall pass away, yet My words remain forever true.
Luke 21:33

42

Lesson 12

✏ Scripture Verse

"He created everything there is — nothing exists that He didn't make." John 1:3

✏ Tip of the Week

How are you holding your pencil? Is it sharp? It is much easier to write well when you hold your pencil correctly and it is sharp!

✏ Letter Focus

Kk, Xx

NOTE:
Directions must be used as part of the Weekly Lesson Format. See page 6.

Lesson 12

TIP OF THE WEEK
How are you holding your pencil?
Is it sharp? It is much easier to write well
when you hold your pencil correctly and it is sharp!

Day One Practice the following letters and words from this week's Scripture.

Kk Kk

Xx Xx

make make

Day Two Continue practicing letters and words from this week's Scripture.

exists exists

created created

43

Extended Teaching

• When students have to rest their writing hand — or shake it because of too much tension — remind them of the correct way to hold the pencil (page 11).

• Suggest students relax the wrist by rotating it in a circle — then reversing the circle. Also have them rotate the shoulders forward and backward.

For Discussion

Have students list three things God created that they especially enjoy. Next, have them share their lists with each other. Ask students, "What do all these wonderful things tell us about how much God loves us?"

Day Three Continue practicing letters and words from this week's Scripture.

nothing

everything

didn't

Day Four Write this week's Scripture verse on a sheet of practice paper.

He created everything
there is — nothing exists that
He didn't make.

John 1:3

44

✏ Scripture Verse

"If anyone wants to be a follower of mine, let him take up his cross and follow Me."
Matthew 16:24

✏ Tip of the Week

The capital T and lowercase † both have a cross, but in different places. Watch where you cross the lowercase †.

✏ Letter Focus

Ss, Tt

NOTE:
Directions must be used as part of the Weekly Lesson Format. See page 6.

Lesson 13

TIP OF THE WEEK
The capital T and lowercase †
both have a cross, but in different
places. Watch where you cross the lowercase †.

Day One Practice the following letters and words from this week's Scripture.

Ss S͞s͞

Tt T͞t͞

wants wants

Day Two Continue practicing letters and words from this week's Scripture.

take take

cross cross

45

✏ Extended Teaching

• Use the letter † as an opportunity to talk of the cross. Suggest that as students write it, they think of how the cross shows God's great love for each of us.

• The capital S and lowercase s are look-alikes. Help students remember formation by showing them the s "begins just below the line and slithers and slinks around the curves."

✏ For Discussion

Ask what "taking up a cross" means to students. Remind them that following Jesus includes doing our very best at whatever task or job God gives us.

Day Three Continue practicing letters and words from this week's Scripture.

let

anyone

mine

Day Four Write this week's Scripture verse on a sheet of practice paper.

If anyone wants to be a follower of mine, let him take up his cross and follow Me. Matthew 16:24

46

Lesson 14

✏ Scripture Verse

"Never criticize or condemn — or it will all come back on you." Luke 6:37

✏ Tip of the Week

Make certain your letters are all the correct size and that they fill the space completely! This makes your writing easier to read.

✏ Letter Focus

Cc, Zz

NOTE:
Directions must be used as part of the Weekly Lesson Format. See page 6.

Lesson 14

TIP OF THE WEEK
Make certain your letters are all the correct size and that they fill the space completely! This makes your writing easier to read.

Day One Practice the following letters and words from this week's Scripture.

Cc Cc

Zz Zz

come come

Day Two Continue practicing letters and words from this week's Scripture.

criticize criticize

back back

47

✏ Extended Teaching

• Ask students, "What number begins like the letter z?" (The number 7) Remind them that except for the 4, numbers zero through nine are written without picking up the pencil.

• Since few words contain the letter z, give the students these extra z words for practice this week: zip, zap, quiz, and zone.

✏ For Discussion

Divide your students into small groups, then have them "Talk about ways that criticizing others can end up hurting you, too." After a short discussion period, have the groups share their answers with the class.

Day Three Continue practicing letters and words from this week's Scripture.

condemn

on

Never

Day Four Write this week's Scripture verse on a sheet of practice paper.

Never criticize or condemn —
or it will all come back on you.
Luke 6:37

48

Scripture Verse

"I came to bring truth to the world. All who love the truth are My followers." John 18:37

Tip of the Week

As you write the lowercase b, be sure to start at the top! Tell a friend exactly how to make this letter.

Letter Focus

Bb, Oo

NOTE:
Directions must be used as part of the Weekly Lesson Format. See page 6.

Lesson 15

Tip of the Week
As you write the lowercase b, be sure to start at the top! Tell a friend exactly how to make this letter.

Day One Practice the following letters and words from this week's Scripture.

Bb Bb

Oo Oo

who who

Day Two Continue practicing letters and words from this week's Scripture.

bring bring

followers followers

49

Extended Teaching

- Use a tall letter with a downstroke to check letter slant. Some tall downstroke letters to help reinforce proper slant are f, h, k, l, and t.

- Have one student verbally describe the lowercase f while another student attempts to write it on the board following their directions. Change students and do it again using the h, k, l, and t.

For Discussion

Ask students "What does it mean to 'love the truth'?" Discuss why honesty is always the best policy.

Day Three Continue practicing letters and words from this week's Scripture.

world   world

truth   truth

came   came

Day Four Write this week's Scripture verse on a sheet of practice paper.

I came to bring truth to the world. All who love the truth are My followers. John 18:37

50

Scripture Verse

"We must worship God, and Him alone. So it is written in the Scriptures." Luke 4:8

Tip of the Week

Two of this week's focus letters are capital and lowercase look-alikes: the S and s; and the W and w. See how the S slithers around?

Letter Focus

Ss, Ww

NOTE:
Directions must be used as part of the Weekly Lesson Format. See page 6.

Lesson 16

TIP OF THE WEEK
Two of this week's focus letters are capital and lowercase look-alikes: the S and s; the W and w. See how the S slithers around?

Day One Practice the following letters and words from this week's Scripture.

Ss

Ww

So

Day Two Continue practicing letters and words from this week's Scripture.

worship

written

51

Extended Teaching

• Start planning early this week on ways to share the Scripture Border Sheet (page 10). Sending the suggested letter on school letterhead helps create good will for the school and positive feedback for the students.

• Encourage students to share experiences from sending Scripture Border Sheets in the past.

For Discussion

Remind students that "worship" includes spending special time with God. Ask them for suggestions on how to do this (prayer, church, reading Scripture stories, etc.).

Day Three Continue practicing letters and words from this week's Scripture.

Scriptures

We

must

Day Four Write this week's Scripture verse on a sheet of practice paper.

We must worship God, and Him alone. So it is written in the Scriptures.

Luke 4:8

52

Scripture Verse

"Praise the Lord, for He has come to visit His people and has redeemed them." Luke 1:68

Tip of the Week

Make good, straight lines for the downstrokes on the capital E, H, L, and P. All these letters are found in this week's lesson.

Letter Focus

Ee, Pp

NOTE:
Directions must be used as part of the Weekly Lesson Format. See page 6.

TIP OF THE WEEK

Make good, straight lines for the downstrokes on the capital E, H, L, and P. All these letters are found in this week's lesson.

Day One   Practice the following letters and words from this week's Scripture.

Ee

Pp

people

Day Two   Continue practicing letters and words from this week's Scripture.

Praise

He

53

Extended Teaching

• Point out the similarities and differences in the focus capital letters. (E, H and L are made with all straight lines. All begin with a downstroke. The L is hidden in the E.)

• Encourage students to watch letter spacing as they write. A letter space is needed between words or practice letters. Remind them that even spacing makes handwriting more readable.

For Discussion

Challenge students to make a list of ways to praise God. You may wish to have them work in small groups. Encourage them to use these ideas to thank God for His love.

Day Three Continue practicing letters and words from this week's Scripture.

them   them

redeemed   redeemed

visit   visit

Day Four Write this week's Scripture verse on a sheet of practice paper.

Praise the Lord, for He has come to visit His people and has redeemed them.

Luke 1:68

54

Lesson 18

✏ Scripture Verse

"I am with you always, even to the end of the world." Matthew 28:20

✏ Tip of the Week

Look around your classroom for a sign that contains the letter ×. (Here's a clue: It should be by the door where you go out.)

✏ Letter Focus

V v, X x

NOTE:
Directions must be used as part of the Weekly Lesson Format. See page 6.

TIP OF THE WEEK

Look around your classroom for a sign that contains the letter **X**. (Here's a clue: It should be by the door where you go out.)

Day One Practice the following letters and words from this week's Scripture.

V v

X x

exit

Day Two Continue practicing letters and words from this week's Scripture.

always

even

55

Extended Teaching

• Encourage students to describe the ∨ and ✕ as they practice them. The ∨ is slant down, slant up, while the ✕ is slant right, slant left.

• Students will enjoy seeing how many body parts they can cross to look like the letter ✕ (fingers, arms, legs — but not eyes, please!).

For Discussion

Ask students what they think God means when He says, "I am with you always." Discuss how God's presence impacts our lives (protection, comfort, security, etc.).

Day Three   Continue practicing letters and words from this week's Scripture.

end

with

the

Day Four   Write this week's Scripture verse on a sheet of practice paper.

I am with you always, even
to the end of the world.
Matthew 28:20

56

Scripture Verse

"God will take care of your tomorrow. Live one day at a time." Matthew 6:34

Tip of the Week

The capital letter A is a three-stroke letter. So are the letters E, F, H, and I. Count the strokes as you write these letters this week.

Letter Focus

A a, L l

NOTE:
Directions must be used as part of the Weekly Lesson Format. See page 6.

Lesson 19

TIP OF THE WEEK
The capital letter A is a three-stroke letter. So are the letters E, F, H, and I. Count the strokes as you write these letters this week.

Day One Practice the following letters and words from this week's Scripture.

A a A a

L l L l

at at

Day Two Continue practicing letters and words from this week's Scripture.

day day

Live Live

57

Extended Teaching

• Have students discuss the similarities and differences between the capital A and X. (Each has two slant down strokes. The A is slant left, slant right; the X is slant right, slant left.)

• Encourage students to write their names carefully. Offer bonus points for any paper that has the student's name written neatly with the correct size letters.

For Discussion

Have students make a list of things that worry them. Now ask them how this text relates to worrying.

Day Three Continue practicing letters and words from this week's Scripture.

time   time

one   one

tomorrow   tomorrow

Day Four Write this week's Scripture verse on a sheet of practice paper.

God will take care of your tomorrow. Live one day at a time. Matthew 6:34

58

Lesson 20

Scripture Verse

"There is joy in the presence of the angels of God when one sinner repents." Luke 15:10

Tip of the Week

If your hand gets tired while you are writing, you may be holding your pencil too tightly. Try to loosen up a bit!

Letter Focus

Tt, Gg

NOTE:
Directions must be used as part of the Weekly Lesson Format. See page 6.

Lesson 20

TIP OF THE WEEK
If your hand gets tired while you are writing, you may be holding your pencil too tightly. Try to loosen up a bit!

Day One   Practice the following letters and words from this week's Scripture.

Tt

Gg

get

Day Two   Continue practicing letters and words from this week's Scripture.

angels

There

59

Extended Teaching

• The † and g are good letters to practice in rhythm. Ask part of the class to sing, "When the Saints Go Marching In," clapping on the first and third beat. Have the rest of the class write the letters to this rhythm. (Start the downstroke or circle on the word "Saints.")

• Challenge students to discover other letters and songs that can be practiced together.

For Discussion

This verse says there is joy in heaven when we repent. Ask students, "What other things can we do that might make God happy?"

Day Three Continue practicing letters and words from this week's Scripture.

presence

repents

when

Day Four Write this week's Scripture verse on a sheet of practice paper.

There is joy in the presence of the angels of God when one sinner repents.
Luke 15:10

60

Scripture Verse

"If you have ears, listen! Be sure to put into practice what you hear." Mark 4:23, 24

Tip of the Week

Some letters are tall, some have tails, and some sit in the middle. But even though your letters are different, they should all be the correct size.

Letter Focus

Ii, Zz

NOTE:
Directions must be used as part of the Weekly Lesson Format. See page 6.

TIP OF THE WEEK
Some letters are tall, some have tails, and some sit in the middle. But even though your letters are different, they should all be the correct size.

Day One Practice the following letters and words from this week's Scripture.

Ii

Zz

size

Day Two Continue practicing letters and words from this week's Scripture.

practice

into

61

Extended Teaching

• Remember to save samples of student writing throughout the year to show progress and note areas for improvement.

• Encourage students to review letters by similar letter practice: tall, tail, circle, two-stroke, etc. (see "Letter Groups," page 161). Note that letters are often included in more than one group.

For Discussion

Read the verse aloud to the students. Ask them what they think Mark is trying to tell us.

Day Three   Continue practicing letters and words from this week's Scripture.

listen   listen

ears   ears

sure   sure

Day Four   Write this week's Scripture verse on a sheet of practice paper.

If you have ears, listen!
Be sure to put into practice
what you hear.
Mark 4:23, 24

62

Scripture Verse

"Your heavenly Father will give the Holy Spirit to those who ask for Him." Luke 11:13

Tip of the Week

Using your index finger, outline a letter on a friend's back. See if they can tell what you wrote. Now trade places and try it again.

Letter Focus

Hh, Yy

NOTE:
Directions must be used as part of the Weekly Lesson Format. See page 6.

Lesson 22

TIP OF THE WEEK
Using your index finger, outline a letter on a friend's back. See if they can tell what you wrote. Now trade places and try it again.

Day One Practice the following letters and words from this week's Scripture.

Hh   Hh

Yy   Yy

Holy   Holy

Day Two Continue practicing letters and words from this week's Scripture.

heavenly   heavenly

Father   Father

63

Extended Teaching

• Ask students to practice curve letters h, m, n, and r. As a letter family there are certain similarities. Encourage students to verbalize these similarities.

• Suggest that students watch for homophones in the practice words this week. (Homophones are words pronounced alike, but different in meaning — like "four" and "for".)

For Discussion

See how many pairs of homophones students can recall (tail, tale; bear, bare; red, read; to, two, too, etc.).

Day Three   Continue practicing letters and words from this week's Scripture.

Your   Your

those   those

ask   ask

Day Four   Write this week's Scripture verse on a sheet of practice paper.

Your heavenly Father will give the Holy Spirit to those who ask for Him. Luke 11:13

64

Scripture Verse

"Blessed are all who hear the Word of God and put it into practice." Luke 11:28

Tip of the Week

How are the capital B and R alike? How are they different? Name some people whose name begins with a B or R.

Letter Focus

Bb, Rr

NOTE:
Directions must be used as part of the Weekly Lesson Format. See page 6.

Lesson 23

TIP OF THE WEEK
How are the capital B and R alike? How are they different? Name some people whose name begins with a B or R.

Day One Practice the following letters and words from this week's Scripture.

Bb

Rr

are

Day Two Continue practicing letters and words from this week's Scripture.

bless

Word

65

Extended Teaching

• Have students describe the ways that the capital B and R are alike. Ask them what other capital letter might fit into this group? (The capital P)

• Ask students to write the tall letter pair b and h, then describe the similarities and differences (page 162).

For Discussion

Have students name some things God asks us to do in Scripture (be kind, love our enemies, help the poor, etc.). Ask them what this verse says will happen if we do what God asks.

Day Three Continue practicing letters and words from this week's Scripture.

Blessed Blessed

who who

hear hear

Day Four Write this week's Scripture verse on a sheet of practice paper.

Blessed are all who hear
the Word of God and put it
into practice.
Luke 11:28

66

Scripture Verse

"Do for others what you want them to do for you." Matthew 7:12

Tip of the Week

Writing is easier if your paper is slanted the same way as your writing arm. This is true not only in handwriting, but in your other subjects as well.

Letter Focus

A a, D d

NOTE:
Directions must be used as part of the Weekly Lesson Format. See page 6.

Lesson 24

TIP OF THE WEEK
Writing is easier if your paper is slanted the same way as your writing arm. This is true not only in handwriting, but in your other subjects as well.

Day One Practice the following letters and words from this week's Scripture.

Aa   Aa

Dd   Dd

Do   Do

Day Two Continue practicing letters and words from this week's Scripture.

want   want

what   what

67

Extended Teaching

• For the left-handed student, note that the paper must slant the same direction as the writing arm. This is very important to prevent an awkward writing hand position.

• Positive comments will help students focus on good posture as they write.

For Discussion

Remind students that this verse is often called "the Golden Rule." Ask them how the world might be different if everyone followed this rule.

Day Three Continue practicing letters and words from this week's Scripture.

to

do

others

Day Four Write this week's Scripture verse on a sheet of practice paper.

Do for others what you
want them to do for you.
Matthew 7:12

68

Lesson 25

Scripture Verse

"God is ready to give blessings to all who come to Him." Luke 4:19

Tip of the Week

If you make a lowercase g with a pipe cleaner or clay, how would you turn it into a q? Write these letters without picking up your pencil.

Letter Focus

Gg, Qq

NOTE:
Directions must be used as part of the Weekly Lesson Format. See page 6.

Lesson 25

TIP OF THE WEEK
If you made a lowercase g with a pipe cleaner or clay, how would you turn it into a q? Write these letters without picking up your pencil.

Day One Practice the following letters and words from this week's Scripture.

Gg

Qq

quit

Day Two Continue practicing letters and words from this week's Scripture.

blessings

God

69

✏ Extended Teaching

• Writing manuscript letters with one stroke (when possible) is vital to helping students make an easier transition to cursive writing. It also diminishes the letter reversal problem.

• Point out that when the students begin cursive writing, the tails of the g and q will extend into the connecting stroke.

✏ For Discussion

Have students make a list of blessings — for each one personally, and the class as a whole. Read some of the blessings aloud. Remind students that blessings surround us, but sometimes we miss them because we're not looking.

Day Three   Continue practicing letters and words from this week's Scripture.

give   give

ready   ready

Him   Him

Day Four   Write this week's Scripture verse on a sheet of practice paper.

God is ready to give blessings to all who come to Him.   Luke 4:19

70

Scripture Verse

"You will know the truth, and the truth will set you free." John 8:32

Tip of the Week

When you sit up straight, it is easier to write and your handwriting improves. When your letters "sit up straight" on the line, they are easier to read.

Letter Focus

Ee, Tt

NOTE:
Directions must be used as part of the Weekly Lesson Format. See page 6.

Lesson 26

TIP OF THE WEEK
When you sit up straight, it is easier to write and your handwriting improves. When your letters "sit up straight" on the line, they are easier to read.

Day One Practice the following letters and words from this week's Scripture.

Ee

Tt

set

Day Two Continue practicing letters and words from this week's Scripture.

free

You

71

Extended Teaching

• Remind students that a slight slant in manuscript writing is acceptable as long as the letter slant is consistent.

• Have students draw a line through some of the tall letters in the practice pages using a different color pencil or crayon. This will help them see if their letters are consistent.

For Discussion

Challenge students to think about someone to share this verse with. Perhaps there's a person in their neighborhood who might be lonely. Suggest that they can make a difference by planning to help just one person this week.

Day Three Continue practicing letters and words from this week's Scripture.

truth

know

will

Day Four Write this week's Scripture verse on a sheet of practice paper.

You will know the truth, and the truth will set you free.
John 8:32

72

Scripture Verse

"If you are friendly only to your friends, how are you different from anyone else?"
Matthew 5:47

Tip of the Week

Two letters in this verse are crossed at the mid-line after the downstroke. Can you find them? (Here's a clue: both are tall letters.)

Letter Focus

F f, M m

NOTE:
Directions must be used as part of the Weekly Lesson Format. See page 6.

TIP OF THE WEEK
Two letters in this verse are crossed at the mid-line after the downstroke. Can you find them? (Here's a clue: both are tall letters.)

Day One Practice the following letters and words from this week's Scripture.

F f   F f

M m   M m

from   from

Day Two Continue practicing letters and words from this week's Scripture.

friends   friends

Matthew   Matthew

73

Extended Teaching

• The two-stroke letters in this verse are f and t. There are more two-stroke letters in manuscript than in cursive. See how many your students can name (f, i, j, k, t, x, and y).

• The capital M is easier to write when it is written with a downstroke. Pick up the pencil, connect to the downstroke, and slant down right, slant up and down.

For Discussion

Who does this verse imply we should be friendly and kind towards? (our enemies, not just our friends) Discuss some ways we can do this.

Day Three Continue practicing letters and words from this week's Scripture.

friendly   friendly

different   different

else   else

Day Four Write this week's Scripture verse on a sheet of practice paper.

If you are friendly only to your friends, how are you different from anyone else? Matthew 5:47

74

Please
Read This
First!

The following 45 practice lessons are designed to be presented one per day for a total of 9 weeks. Before beginning this section, please review the "Making the Transition" on page 4 of this Guidebook.

Please note that Transition lessons (especially Student Workbook pages 77 - 102) should never be used as homework! To maximize each practice session, you must first introduce each new letter to the class, then monitor and encourage the students as they work.

As you present each letter, encourage students to use a variety of practice techniques. Sky Writing, back writing, board practice, verbal descriptions, etc. (see page 154, 162-163) can all help imprint letter formation in the brain. Also, remind students that handwriting is a learned motor skill, and so requires consistent daily practice for mastery.

And don't forget to encourage and *praise* correct letter formation! Creating positive writing experiences now can greatly impact students' future writing success.

To The Teacher

As students begin these Transition lessons, it's important to help them discover the similarities and differences between the manuscript and cursive versions of each letter. This activity helps children form clear mental models of letters and strokes, leading to more accurate letter formation and better handwriting.

Also, many letters in cursive writing use similar patterns in their formation. Be sure to emphasize these similarities by using the information found in the **Cursive Letter Groups** (page 162). This will greatly enhance student understanding as you introduce new letters.

Note: Lessons 1 through 5 introduce the vowels. Since vowels are the most commonly used letters, it's important to master them thoroughly at the start. Lessons 6 through 26 cover the remaining letters in alphabetical order. (After completing Lessons 1 through 26, students have practiced the entire alphabet.) Lessons 27 through 34 are group letter review lessons. Finally, Lessons 35 through 45 are a review of capital and lowercase letters.

 **Transition Lesson 1** *(see Student Workbook, page 77)*

Letter focus A a *𝒜 a*

Directions: Sky Write each letter, verbally describing its formation and pointing out similarities to other cursive letters (see **Cursive Letter Groups**, page 162). Show students how to use the "start dots" and "arrows" as they practice the letters *𝒜 a*. Also, have students practice the lowercase *a* in sets of three to help them master the letter as well as the connecting stroke. Space is given on the first two lines for students to practice their name.

Extended Teaching: While students practice the *a* in sets of three, point out that the lowercase *a* is also a word that can stand alone.

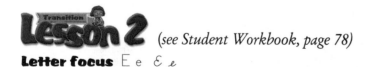 **Transition Lesson 2** *(see Student Workbook, page 78)*

Letter focus E e *ℰ e*

Directions: Sky Write each letter, verbally describing its formation and pointing out similarities to other cursive letters (see **Cursive Letter Groups**, page 162). Encourage students to use the "start dots" and "arrows" as they practice the letters *ℰ e*. Also, have students practice the lowercase *e* in sets of three to help them master the letter as well as the connecting stroke. Space is given on the first two lines for students to practice their name.

Extended Teaching: The vowel *e* is a loop letter. Remind students to leave the loop open — similar to the loop on their shoelace.

Lesson 3 *(see Student Workbook, page 79)*

Letter focus I i ℓ i

Directions: Sky Write each letter, verbally describing its formation and pointing out similarities to other cursive letters (see **Cursive Letter Groups**, page 162). Encourage students to use the "start dots" and "arrows" as they practice the letters ℓ i. Also, have students practice the lowercase i in sets of three to help them master the letter as well as the connecting stroke. Space is given on the first two lines for students to practice their name.

Extended Teaching: Point out that the capital ℓ is also a word that stands alone. Remind students that when the ℓ is used as a word, it's always capitalized.

Lesson 4 *(see Student Workbook, page 80)*

Letter focus O o O o

Directions: Sky Write each letter, verbally describing its formation and pointing out similarities to other cursive letters (see **Cursive Letter Groups**, page 162). Encourage students to use the "start dots" and "arrows" as they practice the letters O o. Also, have students practice the lowercase o in sets of three to help them master the letter as well as the connecting stroke. Space is given on the first two lines for students to practice their name.

Extended Teaching: Several verses in Psalms begin with the letter O. (Example: "O Lord our God, the majesty and glory of your name fills all the earth and overflows the heavens." Psalm 8:1). The modern spelling for that same word is "Oh."

Lesson 5 *(see Student Workbook, page 81)*

Letter focus U u U u

Directions: Sky Write each letter, verbally describing its formation and pointing out similarities to other cursive letters (see **Cursive Letter Groups**, page 162). Encourage students to use the "start dots" and "arrows" as they practice the letters U u. Also, have students practice the lowercase u in sets of three to help them master the letter as well as the connecting stroke. Space is given on the first two lines for students to practice their name.

Extended Teaching: As students write the u in groups of three, remind them to avoid loops and to use clean upstrokes. This takes some practice as the stroke goes up and comes down on the same line.

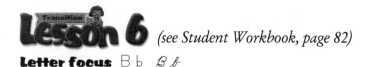 *(see Student Workbook, page 82)*

Letter focus B b $\mathscr{B}$ b

Directions: Sky Write each letter, verbally describing its formation and pointing out similarities to other cursive letters (see **Cursive Letter Groups**, page 162). Encourage students to use the "start dots" and "arrows" as they practice the letters $\mathscr{B}$ b. Also, have students practice the lowercase b in sets of three to help them master the letter as well as the connecting stroke. Space is given on the first two lines for students to practice their name.

Extended Teaching: The lower case b is found in several letter group families. It is a tall letter, a loop letter, an upstroke letter, and a bridgestroke letter. Pointing out letter groups can help students form an accurate mental picture of each letter.

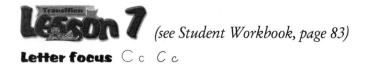 *(see Student Workbook, page 83)*

Letter focus C c $\mathscr{C}$ c

Directions: Sky Write each letter, verbally describing its formation and pointing out similarities to other cursive letters (see **Cursive Letter Groups**, page 162). Encourage students to use the "start dots" and "arrows" as they practice the letters C c. Also, have students practice the lowercase c in sets of three to help them master the letter as well as the connecting stroke. Space is given on the first two lines for students to practice their name.

Extended Teaching: Have students write the word *cab* several times for practice. This will give them practice connecting three letters they have already learned.

 *(see Student Workbook, page 84)*

Letter focus D d $\mathscr{D}$ d

Directions: Sky Write each letter, verbally describing its formation and pointing out similarities to other cursive letters (see **Cursive Letter Groups**, page 162). Encourage students to use the "start dots" and "arrows" as they practice the letters $\mathscr{D}$ d. Also, have students practice the lowercase d in sets of three to help them master the letter as well as the connecting stroke. Space is given on the first two lines for students to practice their name.

Extended Teaching: Have students write the words *dad* and *did* several times for practice. This will give them practice connecting three letters they have already learned.

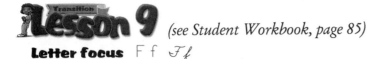 **Lesson 9** *(see Student Workbook, page 85)*

Letter focus F f *Ff*

Directions: Sky Write each letter, verbally describing its formation and pointing out similarities to other cursive letters (see **Cursive Letter Groups**, page 162). Encourage students to use the "start dots" and "arrows" as they practice the letters *Ff*. Also, have students practice the lowercase *f* in sets of three to help them master the letter as well as the connecting stroke. Space is given on the first two lines for students to practice their name.

Extended Teaching: Show students that the lowercase *f* is a tall letter, a loop letter, and a tail letter, and that the capital *F* is a three-stroke letter. Remind students that the downstroke for the capital *F* is written first, then the top line, then the middle cross.

 **Lesson 10** *(see Student Workbook, page 86)*

Letter focus G g *Gg*

Directions: Sky Write each letter, verbally describing its formation and pointing out similarities to other cursive letters (see **Cursive Letter Groups**, page 162). Encourage students to use the "start dots" and "arrows" as they practice the letters *Gg*. Also, have students practice the lowercase *g* in sets of three to help them master the letter as well as the connecting stroke. Space is given on the first two lines for students to practice their name.

Extended Teaching: Show students that the capital *G* is a boatstroke letter that does not connect to the rest of the word. Practice words: *God, bag, gab*

 **Lesson 11** *(see Student Workbook, page 87)*

Letter focus H h *Hh*

Directions: Sky Write each letter, verbally describing its formation and pointing out similarities to other cursive letters (see **Cursive Letter Groups**, page 162). Encourage students to use the "start dots" and "arrows" as they practice the letters *Hh*. Also, have students practice the lowercase *h* in sets of three to help them master the letter as well as the connecting stroke. Space is given on the first two lines for students to practice their name.

Extended Teaching: Remind students that the lowercase *h* is a tall, loop letter. Point out that the capital *H* is a two-stroke capital that starts with a canestroke, then goes down, up and across to connect to the rest of the word. Practice words: *had, hid*

 **Transition Lesson 12** (see Student Workbook, page 88)

Letter focus J j *Jj*

Directions: Sky Write each letter, verbally describing its formation and pointing out similarities to other cursive letters (see **Cursive Letter Groups**, page 162). Encourage students to use the "start dots" and "arrows" as they practice the letters *Jj*. Also, have students practice the lowercase *j* in sets of three to help them master the letter as well as the connecting stroke. Space is given on the first two lines for students to practice their name.

Extended Teaching: Remind students that the lowercase *j* is a two-stroke letter. The dot is added after the word is written. Practice word: *jade*

 **Transition Lesson 13** (see Student Workbook, page 89)

Letter focus K k *Kk*

Directions: Sky Write each letter, verbally describing its formation and pointing out similarities to other cursive letters (see **Cursive Letter Groups**, page 162). Encourage students to use the "start dots" and "arrows" as they practice the letters *Kk*. Also, have students practice the lowercase *k* in sets of three to help them master the letter as well as the connecting stroke. Space is given on the first two lines for students to practice their name.

Extended Teaching: Point out that the capital *K* is a two-stroke capital. The lowercase *k* is a tall, loop letter. Challenge students to discover the similarities between the lowercase *h* and *k* (both are tall, loop letters).

 **Transition Lesson 14** (see Student Workbook, page 90)

Letter focus L l *Ll*

Directions: Sky Write each letter, verbally describing its formation and pointing out similarities to other cursive letters (see **Cursive Letter Groups**, page 162). Encourage students to use the "start dots" and "arrows" as they practice the letters *Ll*. Also, have students practice the lowercase *l* in sets of three to help them master the letter as well as the connecting stroke. Space is given on the first two lines for students to practice their name.

Extended Teaching: The lowercase *l* is another tall, loop letter. Practice words: *fill, hill, jello, lab, leg*

 **Lesson 15** (see Student Workbook, page 91)

Letter focus M m $\mathcal{M}$ m

Directions: Sky Write each letter, verbally describing its formation and pointing out similarities to other cursive letters (see **Cursive Letter Groups**, page 162). Encourage students to use the "start dots" and "arrows" as they practice the letters $\mathcal{M}$ m. Also, have students practice the lowercase m in sets of three to help them master the letter as well as the connecting stroke. Space is given on the first two lines for students to practice their name.

Extended Teaching: The capital $\mathcal{M}$ is a canestroke capital. The word *mom* provides good m practice. Remind students that the words mom and dad are capitalized when used as a name ("I thanked Mom."), but not when used as a simple noun ("I thanked my mom.").

 **Lesson 16** (see Student Workbook, page 92)

Letter focus N n $\mathcal{N}$ n

Directions: Sky Write each letter, verbally describing its formation and pointing out similarities to other cursive letters (see **Cursive Letter Groups**, page 162). Encourage students to use the "start dots" and "arrows" as they practice the letters $\mathcal{N}$ n. Also, have students practice the lowercase n in sets of three to help them master the letter as well as the connecting stroke. Space is given on the first two lines for students to practice their name.

Extended Teaching: Practice words: *man, mine, name*

 **Lesson 17** (see Student Workbook, page 93)

Letter focus P p $\mathcal{P}$ p

Directions: Sky Write each letter, verbally describing its formation and pointing out similarities to other cursive letters (see **Cursive Letter Groups**, page 162). Encourage students to use the "start dots" and "arrows" as they practice the letters $\mathcal{P}$ p. Also, have students practice the lowercase p in sets of three to help them master the letter as well as the connecting stroke. Space is given on the first two lines for students to practice their name.

Extended Teaching: The capital $\mathcal{P}$ is a forward oval capital that begins with a slight upstroke. The lowercase p is a tail letter, as well as an oval letter. Show students that this oval letter does not begin like the lowercase c and a. Practice words: *help, peg, Pam*

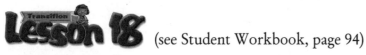 (see Student Workbook, page 94)

Letter focus Q q Q q

Directions: Sky Write each letter, verbally describing its formation and pointing out similarities to other cursive letters (see **Cursive Letter Groups**, page 162). Encourage students to use the "start dots" and "arrows" as they practice the letters Q q. Also, have students practice the lowercase q in sets of three to help them master the letter as well as the connecting stroke. Space is given on the first two lines for students to practice their name.

Extended Teaching: Since the u always tags along with the q, encourage students to practice the qu combination. Practice words: *equip, quack*

 (see Student Workbook, page 95)

Letter focus R r R r

Directions: Sky Write each letter, verbally describing its formation and pointing out similarities to other cursive letters (see **Cursive Letter Groups**, page 162). Encourage students to use the "start dots" and "arrows" as they practice the letters R r. Also, have students practice the lowercase r in sets of three to help them master the letter as well as the connecting stroke. Space is given on the first two lines for students to practice their name.

Extended Teaching: Ask students to look for the similarities between the capital R, P, and B. These three capitals begin alike and have the same first three strokes. R is the only one of these capitals that connects to the rest of the word. Practice words: *ran, run*

 (see Student Workbook, page 96)

Letter focus S s S s

Directions: Sky Write each letter, verbally describing its formation and pointing out similarities to other cursive letters (see **Cursive Letter Groups**, page 162). Encourage students to use the "start dots" and "arrows" as they practice the letters S s. Also, have students practice the lowercase s in sets of three to help them master the letter as well as the connecting stroke. Space is given on the first two lines for students to practice their name.

Extended Teaching: Practice words: *same, sees, sea*

Lesson 21 (see Student Workbook, page 97)

Letter focus T t 𝒯 𝓉

Directions: Sky Write each letter, verbally describing its formation and pointing out similarities to other cursive letters (see **Cursive Letter Groups**, page 162). Encourage students to use the "start dots" and "arrows" as they practice the letters 𝒯 𝓉. Also, have students practice the lowercase 𝓉 in sets of three to help them master the letter as well as the connecting stroke. Space is given on the first two lines for students to practice their name.

Extended Teaching: Point out the boatstroke in the capital 𝒯. Ask students to identify other boatstroke capitals (ℬ, ℱ, 𝒢, ℐ, 𝒮).

Lesson 22 (see Student Workbook, page 98)

Letter focus V v 𝒱 𝓋

Directions: Sky Write each letter, verbally describing its formation and pointing out similarities to other cursive letters (see **Cursive Letter Groups**, page 162). Encourage students to use the "start dots" and "arrows" as they practice the letters 𝒱 𝓋. Also, have students practice the lowercase 𝓋 in sets of three to help them master the letter as well as the connecting stroke. Space is given on the first two lines for students to practice their name.

Extended Teaching: Practice words: *vase, vine, vet*

Lesson 23 (see Student Workbook, page 99)

Letter focus W w 𝒲 𝓌

Directions: Sky Write each letter, verbally describing its formation and pointing out similarities to other cursive letters (see **Cursive Letter Groups**, page 162). Encourage students to use the "start dots" and "arrows" as they practice the letters 𝒲 𝓌. Also, have students practice the lowercase 𝓌 in sets of three to help them master the letter as well as the connecting stroke. Space is given on the first two lines for students to practice their name.

Extended Teaching: Point out the boatstroke in the lowercase 𝓌. Ask students to identify other lowercase letters with boatstrokes (𝒷, 𝑜, 𝓋). Practice words: *bow, book, vow*

 (see Student Workbook, page 100)

Letter focus X x *X x*

Directions: Sky Write each letter, verbally describing its formation and pointing out similarities to other cursive letters (see **Cursive Letter Groups**, page 162). Encourage students to use the "start dots" and "arrows" as they practice the letters *X x*. Also, have students practice the lowercase *x* in sets of three to help them master the letter as well as the connecting stroke. Space is given on the first two lines for students to practice their name.

Extended Teaching: Remind students that the capital and lowercase *x* are both two-stroke letters. Practice words: *exit, exam*

 (see Student Workbook, page 101)

Letter focus Y y *Y y*

Directions: Sky Write each letter, verbally describing its formation and pointing out similarities to other cursive letters (see **Cursive Letter Groups**, page 162). Encourage students to use the "start dots" and "arrows" as they practice the letters *Y y*. Also, have students practice the lowercase *y* in sets of three to help them master the letter as well as the connecting stroke. Space is given on the first two lines for students to practice their name.

Extended Teaching: Point out that the capital and lowercase *Y y* are both tail letters. Practice words: *yet, yellow, yam*

 (see Student Workbook, page 102)

Letter focus Z z *Z z*

Directions: Sky Write each letter, verbally describing its formation and pointing out similarities to other cursive letters (see **Cursive Letter Groups**, page 162). Encourage students to use the "start dots" and "arrows" as they practice the letters *Z z*. Also, have students practice the lowercase *z* in sets of three to help them master the letter as well as the connecting stroke. Space is given on the first two lines for students to practice their name.

Extended Teaching: The capital *Z* is a tail capital. Ask students to identify other tail capitals (*J* and *Y*). The capital *Z* also has a beginning stroke that is very similar to a number. Ask students to identify that number (the 2). Practice words: *zoo, zip*

 **Lesson 27** (see Student Workbook, page 103)

Letter focus: Upstroke letters *e, l, h, k*

Directions: Have students practice the upstroke, loop letters *e, l, h, k*. Remind them to follow the start dots and arrows. Practice word: *help*

Extended Teaching: Remind students to write the *e* with a clear loop. Incorrectly written, the *e* and *i* cause many spelling errors.

 **Lesson 28** (see Student Workbook, page 104)

Letter focus: oval letters *o, a, c, d*

Directions: Have students practice the oval letters *o, a, c, d*. Remind them to follow the start dots and arrows. Practice word: *coal*

Extended Teaching: Point out that carefully closing oval letters will prevent misreading. If the oval is not closed, the *a* can easily be misread as a *u*.

 **Lesson 29** (see Student Workbook, page 105)

Letter focus: oval, tail letters *g, q, p*

Directions: Have students practice the oval tail letters *g, q,* and *p*. Remind them to follow the start dots and arrows. Practice words: *good, equip, gold*

Extended Teaching: Show students the different starting point for the tail letter *p*. Also, point out the differences between the tails of the *g, q,* and *p*.

 **Lesson 30** (see Student Workbook, page 106)

Letter focus: upstroke letters *i, u, w*

Directions: Have students practice the upstroke letters *i, u* and *w*. Remind them to follow the start dots and arrows. Practice words: *with, quick, will*

Extended Teaching: Ask students to find similarities and differences in the three focus letters. (Alike: all begin alike, all are non-loop letters. Different: the *i* is a two-stroke letter, the *w* is a bridgestroke letter, etc.)

 **Lesson 31** (see Student Workbook, page 107)

Letter focus: upstroke letters *j, f, t*

Directions: Have students practice the upstroke, two-stroke letters *j, f, t*. Remind them to follow the start dots and arrows. Practice words: *jump, fit, jet*.

Extended Teaching: Help students see similarities and differences between the tall letter *t*; the tall, tail letter *f*; and the tail letter *j*. Note that some are loop, and some are non-loop strokes.

 **Lesson 32** (see Student Workbook, page 108)

Letter focus: upstroke letters *r, s, b*

Directions: Have students practice the upstroke letters *r, s, b*. Remind them to follow the start dots and arrows. Practice words: *right, sure, boat*

Extended Teaching: Remind students to write the *r* and *s* with distinctive points. Also note the bridgestroke of the *b*. Additional practice words: *bass, rabbits, raspberry*

 **Lesson 33** (see Student Workbook, page 109)

Letter focus: overstroke letters *m, n, v*

Directions: Have students practice the overstroke letters *m, n, v*. Remind them to follow the start dots and arrows. Practice words: *men, jam, verse*

Extended Teaching: Ask students to verbalize how the manuscript m and n are similar to the cursive overstroke *m* and *n*. Additional practice words: *van, many, noon, vat*

 **Lesson 34** (see Student Workbook, page 110)

Letter focus: overstroke letters *x, y, z*

Directions: Have students practice overstroke letters *x, y, z*. Remind them to follow the start dots and arrows. Practice words: *year, zebra, exit*

Extended Teaching: Remind students that the *x* is a two-stroke letter with the second stroke added after the word is written. Additional practice words: *extra, exam, eye, you, yes, zap, zero*

 **Lesson 35** (see Student Workbook, page 111)

Letter focus *Aa, Oo*

Directions: Have students practice *Aa* and *Oo* as well as the three-letter group practice. Remind them that the capital *A* is connected to the rest of the word, but the capital *O* is not. Monitor students' use of start dots and arrows. Practice words: *Abba, Adam, Obadiah, Omega*

Extended Teaching: Some of these words or names may not be familiar to the students. Abba is another name for Father God. Adam was the first man. Obadiah was a prophet from Old Testament times. Omega is the name of the last letter of the Greek alphabet and is also a word that means the last or the end.

 **Lesson 36** (see Student Workbook, page 112)

Letter focus *Cc, Ee*

Directions: Have students practice *Cc* and *Ee* as well as the three-letter group practice. Monitor students' use of start dots and arrows. Practice words: *Caleb, Canaan, Esther, Eve*

Extended Teaching: Help students discover more about these people and places. Caleb and Joshua worked with Moses and were encouragers. Esther was a famous, beautiful queen. Eve was the first woman.

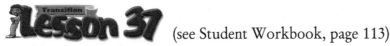 **Lesson 37** (see Student Workbook, page 113)

Letter focus: Boatstroke capitals *Gg, Ss, Tt*

Directions: Have students practice *Gg, Ss, Tt* as well as the three-letter group practice. Monitor students' use of start dots and arrows. As they practice these boatstroke capitals, remind them that boatstroke capitals do not connect to the rest of the word. Practice words: *God, Son, Timothy*

Extended Teaching: Timothy was a young man who traveled with Paul. An interesting view of his life is found in Philippians 2:19-22. Son is capitalized when it refers to God's Son, Jesus.

 **Lesson 38** (see Student Workbook, page 114)

Letter focus Upstroke capitals *Ii, Jj, Qq*

Directions: Have students practice *Ii, Jj, Qq* as well as the three-letter group practice. Monitor students' use of start dots and arrows. Practice words: *Isaac, Jesus, Queen*

Extended Teaching: Isaac was Abraham's promised son. Remind students that queen is not capitalized, except when used as part of a title. (Example: Queen Esther.)

 **Lesson 39** (see Student Workbook, page 115)

Letter focus *Hh, Kk, Xx*

Directions: Have students practice *Hh, Kk,* and *Xx* as well as the three-letter group practice. Monitor students' use of start dots and arrows. Practice words: *Hebrews, Kingdom, Xerxes* (pronounced: zurk' sees)

Extended Teaching: Xerxes does not have an *x* pronunciation, however it does give good *x* practice! Xerxes was a Persian king named in the Old Testament. You'll find his story in the book of Esther. (Note: "Xerxes" is a Greek word. The Hebrew word is "Ahasuerus." Both refer to the same person. Usage in Scripture varies depending on the translation.)

 **Lesson 40** (see Student Workbook, page 116)

Letter focus *Mm, Nn, Uu*

Directions: Have students practice *Mm, Nn,* and *Uu* as well as the three-letter group practice. Monitor students' use of start dots and arrows. Practice words: *Messiah, Numbers, Ur*

Extended Teaching: Numbers is capitalized in this lesson as it refers to a book in the Old Testament. Ur is the early home of Abraham as mentioned in Genesis.

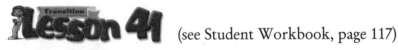 **Lesson 41** (see Student Workbook, page 117)

Letter focus *Ff, Vv, Ww*

Directions: Have students practice *Ff, Vv,* and *Ww* as well as the three-letter group practice. Monitor students' use of start dots and arrows. Practice words: *Father, Victory, Worship*

Extended Teaching: Why would we capitalize the words victory and worship, other than for practice? Challenge students to think of when it's appropriate to capitalize these words. (They're capitalized when they begin a sentence! Examples: Victory is ours in Jesus! Worship the Lord!)

 **Lesson 42** (see Student Workbook, page 118)

Letter focus *D d, L l*

Directions: Have students practice *D d* and *L l* as well as the three-letter group practice. Monitor students' use of start dots and arrows. Practice words: *Daniel, David, Lazarus, Lord*

Extended Teaching: Daniel and David are men mentioned in the Old Testament. The Psalms were written mostly by David. The book Daniel wrote bears his name. Lazarus is the man Jesus raised from the dead. His story is found in John 11:1-12, 19.

 **Lesson 43** (see Student Workbook, page 119)

Letter focus *P p, R r*

Directions: Have students practice *P p* and *R r* as well as the three-letter group practice. Monitor students' use of start dots and arrows. Practice words: *Bible, Paul, Ruth*

Extended Teaching: What are some other words we use for the Bible? (Holy Scriptures, Holy Bible, etc.). Paul is the man who changed his name when God changed his life. Challenge students to discover what his name was before it was Paul (Saul). Ruth is a woman whose story is told in the Old Testament book of that name. She was a very kind, helpful woman.

 **Lesson 44** (see Student Workbook, page 120)

Letter focus *Y y, Z z*

Directions: Have students practice *Y y* and *Z z* as well as the three-letter group practice. Monitor students' use of start dots and arrows. Practice words: *Yoke, You, Zacchaeus, Zion*

Extended Teaching: Not many people are famous because they climbed a tree! Students can read the story of Zacchaeus in Luke 19:1-6.

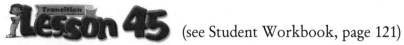 **Transition Lesson 45** (see Student Workbook, page 121)

Letter focus: Alphabet & Number Review

Directions: (read to the student) Write your name on the top line. (pause) Now write the entire alphabet, both capital and lowercase letters, then write all the numbers. Remember your letters should be the correct size and fill the space.

Extended Teaching: Students have now had a thorough introduction and practice of the alphabet, so this makes an excellent post-test. You may want to date and file this page to help evaluate future progress. Remember to praise improvement and to encourage students as they write.

Please Read This First!

Before you begin the daily lessons, please make certain your students clearly understand the following:

> The mechanics of handwriting (see **Proper Positioning**, page 11).
> The format of the class (see **Weekly Lesson Format**, page 8).
> The evaluation process (see **Tips on Grading**, page 9).

It's also very important to have each student write the alphabet (capital and lowercase letters) on a sheet of paper, then sign his or her name and date it. You'll use this sheet later to pinpoint areas of special need, either for individual students, or for the entire class. It's also a good plan to keep this sheet on file to aid in evaluation for the next grading period.

Most importantly, remember that as you acknowledge and reward progress, the learning process is greatly enhanced!

Scripture Verse

"God who began the good work within you will keep right on helping you grow in His grace." Phillipians 1:6

Tip of the Week

As you get taller and smarter this year, make sure your handwriting grows too! Strive to be a **Five Star** student (page 6). Good handwriting helps others read what you have to say.

Letter Focus

Dd, Oo, Yy

NOTE:

Directions must be used as part of the Weekly Lesson Format. See page 6.

TIP OF THE WEEK

As you get taller and smarter this year, make sure your handwriting grows too! Strive to be a **Five Star** student. (See page 6.) Good handwriting helps others read what you have to say.

Day One Practice the following letters and words from this week's Scripture.

Dd

God

good

began

Day Two Continue practicing letters and words from this week's Scripture.

Oo

grow

work

who

125

✏ Extended Teaching

• Review the Five Star evaluation with your students (Student Workbook, page 6). Encourage students to stay aware of these five areas as they write.

• File a dated sample of each student's writing to help you evaluate future progress. Note: It's important to evaluate each student based on his/her own improvement, not just comparison with the model.

✏ For Discussion

How much have you grown since last year? Is physical growth the only way we can grow? What do you think it means to "grow in God's grace"?

Day Three Continue practicing letters and words from this week's Scripture.

Yy

you

grace

will

Day Four Write this week's Scripture verse on a sheet of practice paper.

God who began the good work within you will keep right on helping you grow in His grace.

Phillipians 1:6

FOR DISCUSSION
How much have you grown since last year? Is physical growth the only way we can grow? What do you think it means to "grow in God's grace"?

126

Lesson 2

Scripture Verse

"May God our Father and the Lord Jesus Christ give you all of His blessings, and great peace of heart and mind." I Corinthians 1:3

Tip of the Week

Close your eyes and picture the strokes for the capital and lowercase *Aa, Ee,* and *Jj.* With your eyes still closed, write these six letters with your index finger on the palm of your other hand.

Letter Focus

A a, E e, J j

NOTE:
Directions must be used as part of the Weekly Lesson Format. See page 6.

Lesson 2

TIP OF THE WEEK
Close your eyes and picture the strokes for the capital and lowercase *A a, E e,* and *J j.* With your eyes still closed, write these six letters with your index finger on the palm of your other hand.

Day One   Practice the following letters and words from this week's Scripture.

A a

mind

Father

great

Day Two   Continue practicing letters and words from this week's Scripture.

E e

peace

May

blessings

127

✏ Extended Teaching

• Remind students to be careful as they write the loop in the lowercase *e*. It can easily be mistaken for the non-loop lowercase *i*. Poorly written, these two letters account for many spelling errors.

• Practice the capital letters in this week's lesson: M, G, F, L, J, C. Remind students that the capital M, J, and C connect to the rest of the word.

✏ For Discussion

Make a list of some "blessings" that make you happy. Now compare your list with a friend's. How are they similar. How are they different?

Day Three Continue practicing letters and words from this week's Scripture.

Jj

Jesus

give

heart

Day Four Write this week's Scripture verse on a sheet of practice paper.

May God our Father and the Lord Jesus Christ give you all of His blessings, and great peace of heart and mind.

I Corinthians 1:3

FOR DISCUSSION
Make a list of some "blessings" that make you happy. Now compare your list with a friend's. How are they similar? How are they different?

128

Scripture Verse

"Don't wory about anything; instead, pray about everything; tell God your needs and don't forget to thank Him for His answers."
Phillipians 4:6

Tip of the Week

Letters are different heights, just like people! Some lowercase letters fill only half the space, while tall letters (*b, d, f, h, k, l,* and *t*) fill the whole space, and touch the top lines.

Letter Focus

Rr, Tt, Uu

NOTE:
Directions must be used as part of the Weekly Lesson Format. See page 6.

TIP OF THE WEEK

Letters are different heights, just like people! Some lowercase letters fill only half the space, while tall letters (*b, d, f, h, k, l,* and *t*) fill the whole space, and touch the top lines.

Day One Practice the following letters and words from this week's Scripture.

Rr

worry

pray

answers

Day Two Continue practicing letters and words from this week's Scripture.

Tt

tell

anything

thank

129

✏ Extended Teaching

• Have students practice the *r* combinations from this lesson (*er*, *or*, *ur*, *pr*, and *ry*). Remind them to write the *r* with definite points.

• All the tall letters (*b*, *d*, *f*, *h*, *k*, *l*, *t*) are used in this week's lesson. Remind students that tall letters must touch the top line.

✏ For Discussion

Ask students, "Does God always answer prayers with 'yes'?" "What other answers might God give?" "Why?" Encourage students to share some answers to prayers.

Day Three Continue practicing letters and words from this week's Scripture.

Uu

your

Don't

instead

Day Four Write this week's Scripture verse on a sheet of practice paper.

Don't worry about anything;
instead, pray about everything; tell
God your needs and don't forget to
thank Him for His answers.
Phillipians 4:6

FOR DISCUSSION
Does God always answer prayers with
a "yes"? What other answers
might God give? Why?

130

Lesson 4

✏ Scripture Verse

"Dwell on the fine, good things in others. Think about all you can praise God for and be glad about." Philippians 4:8

✏ Tip of the Week

When you tie your shoes you make loops for the bows. When you write some letters, you use loops, too. Make certain that the loops in *b, e, f, h, k,* and *l* are open — but don't put loops in *t* or *d.*

✏ Letter Focus

$\mathcal{B}\, b,\ \mathcal{L}\, l,\ \mathcal{P}\, p$

NOTE:
Directions must be used as part of the Weekly Lesson Format. See page 6.

Lesson 4

TIP OF THE WEEK

When you tie your shoes, you make loops for the bows.
When you write some letters, you make loops, too! Make certain
the loops in *b, e, f, h, k,* and *l* are open — but don't put loops in *t* or *d.*

Day One   Practice the following letters and words from this week's Scripture.

B b

be

about

dwell

Day Two   Continue practicing letters and words from this week's Scripture.

L l

glad

all

think

131

Extended Teaching

- Students will benefit from Sky Writing the focus letters (see page 154). Sky Writing allows the teacher to see at a glance when students are unsure of letter formation.

- Have students practice the capital $\mathcal{B}$ and $\mathcal{P}$ on practice paper. Point out similarities. Ask students, "What other letter begins like these two letters?" (the $\mathcal{R}$)

For Discussion

What are some of the "fine, good things" that you can see in your classmates? Which of these traits would you like to have, too?

Day Three Continue practicing letters and words from this week's Scripture.

Pp

praise

Phillipians

fine

Day Four Write this week's Scripture verse on a sheet of practice paper.

Dwell on the fine, good things in others. Think about all you can praise God for and be glad about.   Phillipians 4:8

FOR DISCUSSION

What are some of the "fine, good things" that you can see in your classmates? Which of these traits would you like to have, too?

132

Lesson 5

Scripture Verse

"Anyone who believes and says that Jesus is the Son of God has God living in him, and he is living with God." I John 4:15

Tip of the Week

The capital *G* and *S* are boatstroke capitals. The other boatstroke capitals are *B*, *F*, *I* and *T*. Remember, boatstroke capitals are not joined to the rest of the word.

Letter Focus

Gg, Ss, Vv

NOTE:
Directions must be used as part of the Weekly Lesson Format. See page 6.

Tip of the Week

The capitals *G* and *S* are "boatstroke" capitals.
The other boatstroke capitals are *B*, *F*, *I*, and *T*.
Remember, boatstroke capitals are not joined to the rest of the word.

Day One — Practice the following letters and words from this week's Scripture.

Gg

God

anyone

that

Day Two — Continue practicing letters and words from this week's Scripture.

Ss

Son

says

believes

133

Extended Teaching

• As they write this week, remind students to check their letters to make sure they fill the whole space.

• Challenge students to think of someone who needs encouragement (a neighbor, a family member, someone in church). Suggest that they may wish to share their Scripture Border Sheet with that person this week.

For Discussion

When God is living in our hearts, how does this affect our behavior? Name some traits that might show we are "living with God."

Day Three Continue practicing letters and words from this week's Scripture.

Vv

living

him

is

Day Four Write this week's Scripture verse on a sheet of practice paper.

Anyone who believes and says that Jesus is the Son of God has God living in him, and he is living with God.

1 John 4:15

FOR DISCUSSION

When God is living in our hearts, how does this affect our behavior? Name some traits that might show we are "living with God."

134

Scripture Verse

"I can do everything God asks me to with the help of Christ who gives me the strength and power." Phillipians 4:13

Tip of the Week

Is your hand getting tired as you write? You may be holding your pencil incorrectly, or too tightly. Have your teacher check your pencil position. Relax your wrist by rotating it in a circle.

Letter Focus

Cc, Hh, Ww

NOTE:
Directions must be used as part of the Weekly Lesson Format. See page 6.

Lesson 6

TIP OF THE WEEK
Is your hand getting tired as you write? You may be holding your pencil incorrectly, or too tightly. Have your teacher check your pencil position. Relax your wrist by rotating it in a circle.

Day One Practice the following letters and words from this week's Scripture.

Cc

can

Christ

asks

Day Two Continue practicing letters and words from this week's Scripture.

Hh

Help

strength

the

135

Extended Teaching

• It's hard to write smoothly and neatly when you're not relaxed. Encourage your students to breathe deeply and use good posture.

• Remind students that the capital *C* and *H* are connected to the rest of the word. Good practice names include: *Carol*, *Charles*, *Harold*, *Hans*, and *Hannah*. Ask students to check their name to see if the capital letter is connected to the rest of the letters.

For Discussion

What sort of things might God ask you to do? How does this verse say we should get the "strength and power" to do them?

Day Three Continue practicing letters and words from this week's Scripture.

Ww

who

power

with

Day Four Write this week's Scripture verse on a sheet of practice paper.

I can do everything God asks me to with the help of Christ who gives me the strength and power.
Phillipians 4:13

FOR DISCUSSION
What sort of things might God ask you to do? How does this verse say we should get the "strength and power" to do them?

136

Lesson 7

✏ Scripture Verse

"Be kind to each other, tenderhearted, forgiving one another, just as God has forgiven you." Ephesians 4:32

✏ Tip of the Week

There are four lowercase letters (i, j, t, and x) that require an extra stroke after the word is written. Pay close attention to these letters as you practice.

✏ Letter Focus

Ii, Kk, Tt

NOTE:
Directions must be used as part of the Weekly Lesson Format. See page 6.

TIP OF THE WEEK

There are four lowercase letters (i, j, t, and x) that require an extra stroke after the word is written. Pay close attention to these letters as you practice.

Day One Practice the following letters and words from this week's Scripture.

Ii

forgiving

forgiven

just

Day Two Continue practicing letters and words from this week's Scripture.

Kk

kind

has

each

137

✏ Extended Teaching

● Remind students that the focus letters *K* and *T* are two-stroke capital letters. The other two-stroke capitals are *H* and *X*.

● Ask students to find the words in this week's Scripture verse that contain suffixes (tenderhearted, forgiving, forgiven).

✏ For Discussion

List some ways you can show kindness to your classmates. . .your family. . .your neighbors. Try to put at least one of these ideas into action this week.

Day Three Continue practicing letters and words from this week's Scripture.

Tt

tenderhearted

another

other

Day Four Write this week's Scripture verse on a sheet of practice paper.

Be kind to each other, tenderhearted, forgiving one another, just as God has forgiven you.
Ephesians 4:32

FOR DISCUSSION

List some ways you can show kindness to your classmates. . .your family. . .your neighbors. Try to put at least one of these ideas into action this week.

135

Scripture Verse

"Follow God's example in everything you do just as a much loved child imitates his father."
Ephesians 5:1

Tip of the Week

The bridgestroke family includes the lowercase *b*, *o*, *v* and *w*. As you write the connecting stroke, don't let your bridge sag!

Letter Focus

Ff, Mm, Xx

NOTE:
Directions must be used as part of the Weekly Lesson Format. See page 6.

TIP OF THE WEEK
The bridgestroke family includes the lowercase *b*, *o*, *v* and *w*. As you write the connecting stroke, don't let your bridge sag!

Day One Practice the following letters and words from this week's Scripture.

Ff

God's

Follow

his

Day Two Continue practicing letters and words from this week's Scripture.

Mm

imitates

much

child

139

Extended Teaching

- Show students that the capital $\mathcal{F}$ is the only three-stroke capital. Encourage students to practice this letter on the board while counting 1-2-3.

- Since there are very few words that contain an x, here are some extra words to practice: *extreme, exact, exit, except.*

For Discussion

What are some good ways we might imitate God? Watch for opportunities to put these into practice!

Day Three   Continue practicing letters and words from this week's Scripture.

Xx

example

everything

loved

Day Four   Write this week's Scripture verse on a sheet of practice paper.

Follow God's example in everything you do just as a much loved child imitates his father.

Ephesians 5:1

FOR DISCUSSION

What are some good ways we might imitate God? Watch for opportunities to put these into practice!

140

Lesson 9

✏ Scripture Verse

"Let everyone be sure that he is doing his very best, for then he will have the personal satisfaction of work well done." Galatians 6:4

✏ Tip of the Week

A train won't work unless it's on the track. Keep your handwriting on track by making sure your letters rest firmly on the line.

✏ Letter Focus

A a, L l, R r

NOTE:
Directions must be used as part of the Weekly Lesson Format. See page 6.

Lesson 9

TIP OF THE WEEK
A train won't work unless it's on the track. Keep your handwriting on track this week by making sure your letters rest firmly on the line.

Day One Practice the following letters and words from this week's Scripture.

A a

have

Galatians

satisfaction

Day Two Continue practicing letters and words from this week's Scripture.

L l

personal

well

Let

141

Extended Teaching

- Review the Five Star evaluation with the students. Encourage them to demonstrate each "star" on the board, showing what is good practice and what it isn't. (See Student Workbook, page 6.) Ask them to identify at least one area of the five that they could improve in.

- The capital $\mathcal{L}$ is a downstroke capital. Have students look for the similar stroke in the capital $\mathcal{D}$.

For Discussion

Why is it important to always do your very best? Make a list of some areas you'd like to improve in. Don't forget to ask God to help you!

Day Three Continue practicing letters and words from this week's Scripture.

Rr

work

sure

best

Day Four Write this week's Scripture verse on a sheet of practice paper.

Let everyone be sure that he is doing his very best, for then he will have the personal satisfaction of work well done.

Galatians 6:4

FOR DISCUSSION
Why is it important to always do your very best? Make a list of some areas you'd like to improve in. Don't forget to ask God to help you!

142

Scripture Verse

"Most important of all, continue to show deep love for each other, for love makes up for many of your faults." I Peter 4:8

Tip of the Week

This verse contains most of the overstroke letters (m, n, v, y). Think of some words that contain the other overstroke letters (x and z) and practice them, too!

Letter Focus

Mm, Nn, Oo

NOTE:
Directions must be used as part of the Weekly Lesson Format. See page 6.

Lesson 10

TIP OF THE WEEK
This verse contains most of the overstroke letters (m, n, v, y). Think of some words that contain the other overstroke letters (x and z) and practice them, too!

Day One Practice the following letters and words from this week's Scripture.

Mm

Most

important

makes

Day Two Continue practicing letters and words from this week's Scripture.

Nn

continue

many

deep

143

Extended Teaching

• Remind students to leave a letter space between their words as they write.

• Practice words that contain overstroke letters are *man*, *yes*, *excuse*, *extra*, *zip*, and *zone*. Ask students to check these words carefully for correct letter formation.

For Discussion

Why is it so important for Christians to love one another? (Have students read John 13:34, 35. "Love each other just as much as I love you. Your strong love for each other will prove to the world that you are my disciples.")

Day Three Continue practicing letters and words from this week's Scripture.

Oo

other

show

faults

Day Four Write this week's Scripture verse on a sheet of practice paper.

Most important of all, continue to show deep love for each other, for love makes up for many of your faults.

I Peter 4:8

FOR DISCUSSION
Why is it so important for Christians to love one another? (Hint: see John 13:34, 35.)

144

Scripture Verse

"God has given each of you some special abilities; be sure to use them to help each other." I Peter 4:10

Tip of the Week

Just like the capital C, the oval capital E begins just below the top line. Also, remember that the forward oval capitals B, P, and R begin with a "flagstroke." (Notice the flagpole is leaning a bit!)

Letter Focus

Ee, Pp, Ss

NOTE:
Directions must be used as part of the Weekly Lesson Format. See page 6.

Lesson 11

TIP OF THE WEEK
Just like the capital C, the oval capital E begins just below the top line. Also, remember that the forward oval capitals B, P, and R begin with a flagstroke. (Notice the flagpole is leaning a bit!)

Day One Practice the following letters and words from this week's Scripture.

Ee

each

given

abilities

Day Two Continue practicing letters and words from this week's Scripture.

Pp
Peter

help

special

145

Extended Teaching

• Encourage students to write numbers with one stroke (except for the number *4*).

• Special letter combinations to practice this week are *ch*, *sp*, *ab*, *th*, *lp*, and *al*. Remind students that the connecting stroke in all these combinations needs to touch the baseline.

For Discussion

What special ability, knowledge, or talent has God given you? List some things that all of us can do to be helpful.

Day Three Continue practicing letters and words from this week's Scripture.

Ss

some

sure

use

Day Four Write this week's Scripture verse on a sheet of practice paper.

God has given each of you some special abilities; be sure to use them to help each other.

I Peter 4:10

For Discussion
What special ability, knowledge, or talent has God given you? List some things that all of us can do to be helpful.

146

Scripture Verse

"The Lord is watching His children, listening to their prayers." I Peter 3:12

Tip of the Week

The *H*, *T*, and *K* are two-stroke capital letters. There is also one three-stroke capital letter. Can you guess what it is? Here's a hint: It's just like a *T*, but with one stroke more (the letter *F*).

Letter Focus

Hh, Ll, Tt

NOTE:

Directions must be used as part of the Weekly Lesson Format. See page 6.

Lesson 12

TIP OF THE WEEK

The *H*, *T*, and *K*, are two-stroke capital letters.
There is also one three-stroke capital letter. Can you guess
what it is? (Here's a hint: It's just like a *T*, but with one stroke more.)

Day One   Practice the following letters and words from this week's Scripture.

Hh

His

their

prayers

Day Two   Continue practicing letters and words from this week's Scripture.

Ll

Lord

children

listening

147

Extended Teaching

• Challenge students to write the Evaluation Sentence (page 9) as many times as possible in one minute. Students should work on speed, but without sacrificing legibility.

• Suggest that students relax their wrists by doing circle wrist exercises before writing. This will help them write more smoothly.

For Discussion

Having someone watch us can make us feel very good. But sometimes it makes us feel bad. What are some possible reasons for this? (Sometimes it depends on why people are watching — to see how good we are doing, or to criticize us.)

Day Three Continue practicing letters and words from this week's Scripture.

It

The

to

watching

Day Four Write this week's Scripture verse on a sheet of practice paper.

The Lord is watching His children, listening to their prayers.
I Peter 3:12

FOR DISCUSSION
Having someone watch us can make us feel very good. But sometimes it makes us feel bad. What are some possible reasons for this?

148

Scripture Verse

"Be beautiful inside, in your hearts, with the lasting charm of a gentle and quiet spirit which is so precious to God." I Peter 3:4

Tip of the Week

The lowercase *g* and *q* are very similar. Be certain you know which way the tail goes for each. The *q* is usually found beside its best friend, the *u*. Practice the *qu* combination.

Letter Focus

Bb, Gg, Qq

NOTE:
Directions must be used as part of the Weekly Lesson Format. See page 6.

Lesson 13

TIP OF THE WEEK
The lowercase *g* and *q* are very similar. Be certain you know which way the tail goes for each. The *q* is usually found beside its best friend, the *u*. Practice the *qu* combination this week.

Day One Practice the following letters and words from this week's Scripture.

Bb

Be

beautiful

inside

Day Two Continue practicing letters and words from this week's Scripture.

Gg

gentle

lasting

precious

149

Extended Teaching

- Have students practice the tail letters from this week's verse (*f*, *g*, *p*, *q*, and *y*). Remind them that practicing *any* letter in a set of three improves both the letter *and* the connecting stroke.

- Remind students that what we're really like on the inside isn't visible in a mirror — but is visible to God. Ask, "What's something you can do today to develop inner beauty?"

For Discussion

Can someone be pretty on the outside, but ugly on the inside? How about the opposite? Explain. (The way we act often shows what we are really like inside.)

Day Three Continue practicing letters and words from this week's Scripture.

Qq

quiet

spirit

charm

Day Four Write this week's Scripture verse on a sheet of practice paper.

Be beautiful inside, in your hearts, with the lasting charm of a gentle and quiet spirit which is so precious to God.

I Peter 3:4

FOR DISCUSSION

Can someone be pretty on the outside, but ugly on the inside? How about the opposite? Explain.

150

Lesson 14

Scripture Verse

"You should be like one big happy family, full of sympathy toward each other, loving one another with tender hearts and humble minds."
I Peter 3:8

Tip of the Week

Everyone's name is special. You may be named after a relative, a family friend, or something totally unique! Be proud of your name and write it so anyone can read it.

Letter Focus

Oo, Uu, Yy

NOTE:
Directions must be used as part of the Weekly Lesson Format. See page 6.

Lesson 14

TIP OF THE WEEK
Everyone's name is special. You may be named
after a relative, or family friend, or something totally unique!
Be proud of your name and write it so anyone can read it!

Day One Practice the following letters and words from this week's Scripture.

Oo

loving

one

toward

Day Two Continue practicing letters and words from this week's Scripture.

Uu

humble

should

tender

151

Extended Teaching

• Point out that the capital letters *Y* and *U* both begin with a canestroke. Ask students to identify other canestroke capitals (*K, M, N, V, W,* and *X*).

• This is a good verse to practice in manuscript. Manuscript handwriting is a life skill, so it is an important ability to maintain.

For Discussion

When someone you care about feels bad, do you feel bad, too? How does this relate to our Scripture verse this week?

Day Three   Continue practicing letters and words from this week's Scripture.

Yy

family

sympathy

minds

Day Four   Write this week's Scripture verse on a sheet of practice paper.

You should be like one big happy family, full of sympathy toward each other, loving one another with tender hearts and humble minds.

I Peter 3:8

FOR DISCUSSION
When someone you care about feels bad, do you feel bad, too? How does this relate to our Scripture verse this week?

152

Scripture Verse

"If we are living in the light of God's presence . . . we have wonderful fellowship and joy with each other." I John 1:7

Tip of the Week

There are two dotted letters this week—the *i* and *j*. Add a small dot (not a circle) after you finish the word. Also, check your lowercase *e*'s to make sure they don't look like *i*'s.

Letter Focus

Ff, Ii, Jj

NOTE:
Directions must be used as part of the Weekly Lesson Format. See page 6.

TIP OF THE WEEK

There are two dotted letters this week — the *i* and *j*.
Add a small dot (not a circle) after you finish the word. Also,
check your lowercase *e*'s to make sure they don't look like *i*'s.

Day One   Practice the following letters and words from this week's Scripture.

Ff

fellowship

wonderful

we

Day Two   Continue practicing letters and words from this week's Scripture.

Ii

Jj

light

living

153

Extended Teaching

- Remind students that incorrectly written *e*'s and *i*'s account for many spelling errors.

- Point out the ellipsis (…) in this verse, and explain that it means some words were left out.

- This lesson has a number of tricky bridgestroke *w* connections. Pay close attention to *we*, *wo*, *ows*, and *wi*.

For Discussion

According to this verse, how does our relationship with God affect the way we relate to each other? Explain.

Day Three Continue practicing letters and words from this week's Scripture.

Jj

John

joy

presence

Day Four Write this week's Scripture verse on a sheet of practice paper.

If we are living in the light of God's presence… we have wonderful fellowship and joy with each other.

I John 1:7

FOR DISCUSSION

According to this verse, how does our relationship with God affect the way we relate to each other? Explain.

154

Scripture Verse

"Don't repay evil for evil. Don't snap back at those who say unkind things about you. . .We are to be kind to others, and God will bless us for it." I Peter 3:9

Tip of the Week

Your lowercase oval letters (a, c, d, g, o, and q) should be round and smooth, not squashed like someone sat on them! To look its best, the oval part of each letter should fill the middle space.

Letter Focus

A a, D d, R r

NOTE:
Directions must be used as part of the Weekly Lesson Format. See page 6.

Lesson 16

TIP OF THE WEEK
Your lowercase oval letters (a, c, d, g, o, and q) should be round and smooth, not squashed like someone sat on them! To look its best, the oval part of each letter should fill the middle space.

Day One Practice the following letters and words from this week's Scripture.

A a

snap

are

at

Day Two Continue practicing letters and words from this week's Scripture.

D d

Don't

unkind

evil

155

Extended Teaching

• A few extra *q* words to practice this week are *quick*, *quart*, and *quiz*.

• Have students categorize the lowercase letters into loop and non-loop letters. To sharpen their writing skills, have them practice any difficult letters in sets of three.

For Discussion

How should you act when someone is being unkind? What should be our attitude toward those who are mean to us? Hint: see Luke 23:34. ("Father, forgive these people," Jesus said, "for they don't know what they are doing.")

Day Three   Continue practicing letters and words from this week's Scripture.

Rr

repay

those

back

Day Four   Write this week's Scripture verse on a sheet of practice paper.

Don't repay evil for evil.
Don't snap back at those who say
unkind things about you...We are
to be kind to others, and God will
bless us for it.
I Peter 3:9

FOR DISCUSSION
How should you act when someone is being unkind? What should be our attitude toward those who are mean to us? (Hint: see Luke 23:34.)

156

Scripture Verse

"I pray that Christ will be more and more at home in your hearts, living within you as you trust in Him." Ephesians 3:17

Tip of the Week

Just as you need space between a classmate's desk and your desk, so words need a letter space between them for easier reading. Wordsthatare tooclosetogether are much too hard to read!

Letter Focus

Hh, Ss, Uu

NOTE:
Directions must be used as part of the Weekly Lesson Format. See page 6.

TIP OF THE WEEK

Just as you need space between a classmate's desk and your desk, so words need a letter space between them for easier reading. Wordsthataretooclosetogether are much too hard to read!

Day One Practice the following letters and words from this week's Scripture.

Hh

home

within

that

Day Two Continue practicing letters and words from this week's Scripture.

Ss

hearts

as

trust

157

✏ Extended Teaching

● Have students practice the canestroke capitals *H* and *V*.

● Point out that the capital *H* is connected to the rest of the letters in the word. Some words to practice are *He*, *Him*, and *His*.

● Many New Testament books were written by Paul. Have students check first verses of the Epistles (Romans to Philemon) for clues.

✏ For Discussion

What does it mean to make someone "feel at home"? Describe the kind of heart where Jesus could feel at home.

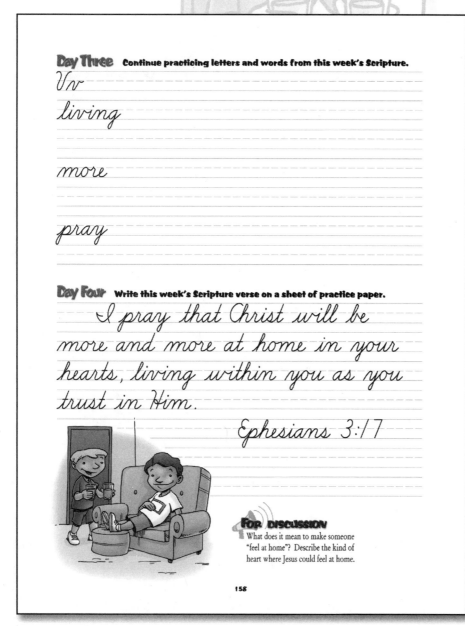

Day Three Continue practicing letters and words from this week's Scripture.

Vv

living

more

pray

Day Four Write this week's Scripture verse on a sheet of practice paper.

I pray that Christ will be more and more at home in your hearts, living within you as you trust in Him.

Ephesians 3:17

FOR DISCUSSION
What does it mean to make someone "feel at home"? Describe the kind of heart where Jesus could feel at home.

158

Scripture Verse

"God is at work within you, helping you want to obey Him, and then helping you do what He wants." Philippians 2:13

Tip of the Week

Look for the similarities and differences between the lowercase *u - w*; and the *m - n*. Make certain you write these letters clearly and carefully so they can't be mistaken for each other.

Letter Focus

Nn, Pp, Ww

NOTE:
Directions must be used as part of the Weekly Lesson Format. See page 6.

Lesson 18

TIP OF THE WEEK
Look for similarities and differences between the lowercase *u-w*; and the *m-n*. Make certain you write these letters clearly and carefully so they can't be mistaken for each other.

Day One   Practice the following letters and words from this week's Scripture.

Nn

and

then

wants

Day Two   Continue practicing letters and words from this week's Scripture.

Pp
Philippians

helping

obey

159

Extended Teaching

• This week's verse contains several *n*'s and *w*'s. They're almost the reverse of each other. Remind students that the *w* connecting stroke is a bridgestroke.

• Helpful letter combinations to practice this week are *wo, wi, wa*, and *wh*.

• Remind students that a sharp pencil makes writing much easier to read.

For Discussion

Where does this verse say the desire to obey comes from? List some ways that we can become closer to God.

Day Three   Continue practicing letters and words from this week's Scripture.

Ww

want

work

what

Day Four   Write this week's Scripture verse on a sheet of practice paper.

God is at work within you, helping you want to obey Him, and then helping you do what He wants.

Philippians 2:13

FOR DISCUSSION

Where does this verse say the desire to obey comes from? List some ways that we can become closer to God.

160

Scripture Verse

"May you always be doing those good, kind things which show that you are a child of God, for this will bring much praise and glory to the Lord." Philippians 1:11

Tip of the Week

Look for similarities and differences between the lowercase *h* and *k*. Like the lowercase *u* - *w* and *m* - *n*, these letters must be written clearly to avoid mistakes in reading.

Letter Focus

Bb, Gg, Kk

NOTE:
Directions must be used as part of the Weekly Lesson Format. See page 6.

Lesson 19

TIP OF THE WEEK

Look for similarities and differences between the lowercase *h* and *k*. Like the lowercase *u* - *w* and *m* - *n*, these letters must be written clearly to avoid mistakes in reading.

Day One   Practice the following letters and words from this week's Scripture.

Bb

bring

be

child

Day Two   Continue practicing letters and words from this week's Scripture.

Gg

good

glory

which

161

✏ Extended Teaching

• Remind students that tall letters should touch the top line. The letters *b*, *h*, *k*, and *l* contain a similar loop. Good words to practice are *hike*, *bill*, and *bike*.

• Remind students that the canestroke capital *K* is made with two strokes. It's a letter that is connected to the rest of the word. A good practice word is *King*.

✏ For Discussion

List some ways we can help our neighbors. How does our kind behavior affect what people think about Christians?

Day Three Continue practicing letters and words from this week's Scripture.

K k

kind

doing

praise

Day Four Write this week's Scripture verse on a sheet of practice paper.

May you always be doing those good, kind things which show that you are a child of God, for this will bring much praise and glory to the Lord.

Philippians 1:11

For Discussion

List some ways we can help our neighbors. How does our kind behavior affect what people think about Christians?

162

Scripture Verse

"Be gentle and ready to forgive; never hold grudges. Remember, the Lord forgave you, so you must forgive others." Colossians 3:13

Tip of the Week

Have you looked at the "stars" lately? The **Five Star** evaluation can help you determine areas in your handwriting that need work. Watch your alignment, shape, size, slant, and spacing.

Letter Focus

Dd, Ee, Ff

NOTE:
Directions must be used as part of the Weekly Lesson Format. See page 6.

Lesson 20

TIP OF THE WEEK

Have you looked at the "stars" lately? The **Five Star** evaluation can help you determine areas in your handwriting that need work. Watch your alignment, shape, size, slant and spacing.

Day One Practice the following letters and words from this week's Scripture.

Dd

grudges

ready

hold

Day Two Continue practicing letters and words from this week's Scripture.

Ee

Remember

gentle

never

163

Extended Teaching

- Review the **Five Star** evaluation. Using the board, let students show an exaggerated example of what *not* to do for each of the five areas. This helps students focus on the *true* goals.

- This week's verse is similar to "The Golden Rule" (Matthew 7:12). Read Matthew 6:12 aloud, then encourage students to think of someone they need to forgive. Remind them God forgives us as we forgive others.

For Discussion

How can holding a grudge be harmful? Why do you think forgiving each other is important?

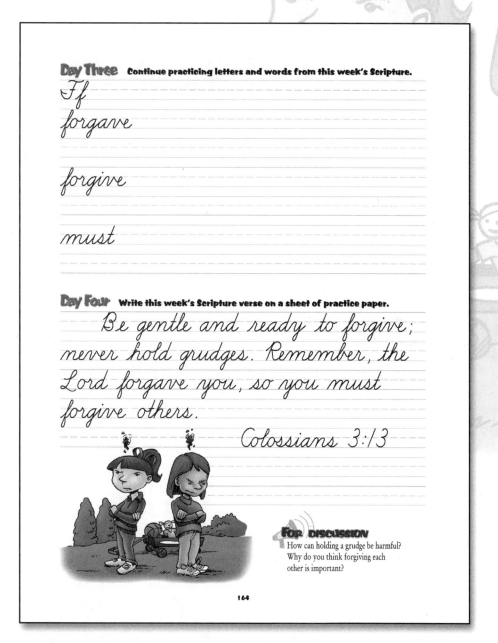

Day Three Continue practicing letters and words from this week's Scripture.

Ff

forgave

forgive

must

Day Four Write this week's Scripture verse on a sheet of practice paper.

Be gentle and ready to forgive; never hold grudges. Remember, the Lord forgave you, so you must forgive others.

Colossians 3:13

FOR DISCUSSION
How can holding a grudge be harmful? Why do you think forgiving each other is important?

164

Lesson 21

✏ Scripture Verse

"Most of all, let love guide your life, for then the whole church will stay together in perfect harmony." Colossians 3:14

✏ Tip of the Week

Some of us look a lot like our parents. Some capital and lowercase pairs look alike too! The *Cc* is one such pair. Also look at the *Aa*, *Xx*, *Yy*, and *Zz*.

✏ Letter Focus

Cc, Ll, Mm

NOTE:
Directions must be used as part of the Weekly Lesson Format. See page 6.

TIP OF THE WEEK
Some of us look a lot like our parents. Some capital and lowercase pairs look alike, too. The *Cc* is one such pair. Also look at the *Aa*, *Xx*, *Yy*, *Zz*.

Day One Practice the following letters and words from this week's Scripture.

Cc

Colossians

church

perfect

Day Two Continue practicing letters and words from this week's Scripture.

Ll

life

let

whole

165

Extended Teaching

• Have students identify and practice the similar down stroke in the capital *L* and *D*.

• As your students practice the *c*, add the oval letter *o* (same letter family). Remind them that the *o* connecting bridgestroke doesn't touch the baseline. Challenging letter combinations in this verse to practice are *os, of, ov, ou, or, ol* and *og*.

For Discussion

If you really love everyone, how might it affect your behavior? List some ways you can let love guide your life.

Day Three Continue practicing letters and words from this week's Scripture.

Mm

Most

harmony

all

Day Four Write this week's Scripture verse on a sheet of practice paper.

Most of all, let love guide your life, for then the whole church will stay together in perfect harmony.

Colossians 3:14

FOR DISCUSSION
If you really love everyone, how might it affect your behavior? List some ways you can let love guide your life.

166

Lesson 22

✏ Scripture Verse

"But the wisdom that comes from heaven is first of all pure and full of quiet gentleness. Then it is peace-loving and courteous." James 3:17

✏ Tip of the Week

To help you remember the correct strokes, Sky Write the capital letters from this lesson (*Ii, Jj,* and *Q*), and see if a classmate can tell which one you're writing!

✏ Letter Focus

Ii, Jj, Qq

NOTE:
Directions must be used as part of the Weekly Lesson Format. See page 6.

TIP OF THE WEEK
To help you remember the correct strokes, skywrite the capital letters from this lesson (*Ii, Jj,* and *Q*) and see if a classmate can tell which one you're writing.

Day One   Practice the following letters and words from this week's Scripture.

Ii

first

loving

comes

Day Two   Continue practicing letters and words from this week's Scripture.

Jj

James

peace

pure

167

Extended Teaching

• Allow students to practice writing the three upswing capitals (*I*, *J*, *Q*) on the board. Large strokes will help imprint the formation of these letters firmly in the brain. It's a challenge to keep the slant consistent.

• Suggest that students practice the tail letters (*f*, *g*, *j*, *p*, *q*, *y* and *z*), remembering that they touch the baseline.

For Discussion

Think of someone who seems "full of quiet gentleness." How do you think they became that kind of person?

Day Three Continue practicing letters and words from this week's Scripture.

Qq

quiet

heaven

gentleness

Day Four Write this week's Scripture verse on a sheet of practice paper.

But the wisdom that comes
from heaven is first of all pure
and full of quiet gentleness. Then
it is peace—loving and courteous.
James 3:17

FOR DISCUSSION
Think of someone who seems "full of quiet gentleness." How do you think they became that kind of person?

168

Scripture Verse

"Be patient with each other, making allowance for each other's faults because of your love."
Ephesians 4:2

Tip of the Week

Check your posture. It's amazing how much difference correct posture can make in your handwriting. Also, make sure your paper is going the same direction as your writing arm.

Letter Focus

Kk, Uu, Xx

NOTE:
Directions must be used as part of the Weekly Lesson Format. See page 6.

TIP OF THE WEEK

Check your posture. It's amazing how much
difference correct posture can make in your handwriting. Also,
make sure your paper is going the same direction as your writing arm.

Day One   Practice the following letters and words from this week's Scripture.

Kk

making

make

other's

Day Two   Continue practicing letters and words from this week's Scripture.

Uu

faults

because

each

169

Extended Teaching

• Remind students that whether they write with the right or left hand, it's easier to keep a consistent slant when the paper is going the same direction as their writing arm.

• Expand students' vocabulary by discussing the several meanings of the word "allowance": 1) To make allowance for, to forgive; 2) A sum of money "allowed" or granted for a particular purpose; 3) A reduction in price.

For Discussion

Have you ever been impatient with someone, or critical? How can we learn to make allowances for another's weaknesses?

Day Three   Continue practicing letters and words from this week's Scripture.

Xx

exception

allowance

patient

Day Four   Write this week's Scripture verse on a sheet of practice paper.

Be patient with each other, making allowance for each other's faults because of your love.

Ephesians 4:2

FOR DISCUSSION

Have you ever been impatient with someone, or critical? How can we learn to make allowances for another's weaknesses?

170

Lesson 24

✏ Scripture Verse

"You are members of God's very own family, citizens of God's country, and you belong in God's household with every other Christian."
Ephesians 2:19

✏ Tip of the Week

The apostrophe *s* on *God's* means we belong to God — we're part of God's family! To care for the rest of the family, share your Scripture Border Sheet with someone new this week.

✏ Letter Focus

Cc, Yy, Zz

NOTE:
Directions must be used as part of the Weekly Lesson Format. See page 6.

Lesson 24

TIP OF THE WEEK
The apostrophe *s* on *God's* means we belong to God — we're part of God's family! To care for the rest of the family, share your Scripture Border Sheet with someone new this week.

Day One Practice the following letters and words from this week's Scripture.

Cc

Christian

country

belong

Day Two Continue practicing letters and words from this week's Scripture.

Yy
You

family

members

171

Extended Teaching

• Point out the punctuation in this week's verse (apostrophes, comma, period, and colon). Remind students that a colon is always used between the numbers in a Scripture text to show chapter and verse.

• Explore the concept of being a member of "God's family." What does this mean? How should it affect our relationship with others?

For Discussion

Isn't it great to be part of God's family? List some ways that you can share God's love with others.

Day Three Continue practicing letters and words from this week's Scripture.

Zz

citizens

household

God's

Day Four Write this week's Scripture verse on a sheet of practice paper.

You are members of God's very own family, citizens of God's country, and you belong in God's household with every other Christian.

Ephesians 2:19

FOR DISCUSSION
Isn't it great to be part of God's family?
List some ways you can share
God's love with others.

172

✎ Scripture Verse

"May your roots go down deep into the soil of God's marvelous love; and may you be able to feel and understand. . .how long, how wide, how deep, and how high His love really is."
Ephesians 3:17-19

✎ Tip of the Week

Make sure your letters are "planted" in the right space. Your tail letters need to touch the bottom line, and your tall letters need to reach the top line.

✎ Letter Focus

Mm, Oo, Ww

NOTE:
Directions must be used as part of the Weekly Lesson Format. See page 6.

TIP OF THE WEEK
Make sure your letters are "planted" in the right space. Your tail letters need to touch the bottom line, and your tall letters need to reach the top line.

Day One Practice the following letters and words from this week's Scripture.

Mm

May

marvelous

high

Day Two Continue practicing letters and words from this week's Scripture.

Oo

down

soil

roots

173

Extended Teaching

• Encourage students to classify all the lower-case alphabet into groups. (See page 162 for letter group names.) Remind students that letters may be in more than one group.

• Bring a live plant to class and show students the root structure. Remind them that as roots expand, they draw in more nourishment. In the same way, as our understanding of God's love expands it helps us grow spiritually.

For Discussion

What do you think this verse means when it says our "roots" should "go down deep" into God's love? Explain.

Day Three Continue practicing letters and words from this week's Scripture.

Ww

how

wide

understand

Day Four Write this week's Scripture verse on a sheet of practice paper.

May your roots go down deep into the soil of God's marvelous love; and may you be able to feel and understand.. how long, how wide, how deep, and how high His love really is.

Ephesians 3:17-19

For Discussion
What do you think this verse means when it says our "roots" should "go down deep" into God's love? Explain.

174

✏ Scripture Verse

"May the Lord bring you into an ever deeper understanding of the love of God and of the patience that comes from Christ."
II Thessalonians 3:5

✏ Tip of the Week

Remember, to help you write more rapidly and smoothly, dot your *i*'s and cross your *t*'s *after* you finish the entire word. The same is true for *j*'s and *x*'s, too.

✏ Letter Focus

Gg, Rr, Tt

NOTE:
Directions must be used as part of the Weekly Lesson Format. See page 6.

TIP OF THE WEEK

Remember, to help you write more rapidly and smoothly, be sure to dot your *i*'s and cross your *t*'s *after* you finish the entire word. The same is true for *j*'s and *x*'s, too.

Day One   Practice the following letters and words from this week's Scripture.

Gg

God

bring

understanding

Day Two   Continue practicing letters and words from this week's Scripture.

Rr

ever

deeper

from

175

Extended Teaching

• Have students identify words with special word endings (*ing*, *s*, *ed*, *er*) in this week's verse.

• Encourage students to talk about ways to demonstrate patience. Remind them that patience is not just sitting and waiting — it's cheerfully doing what God has given you to do *today*, while waiting for circumstances to change.

For Discussion

What have you learned about the love of God this year? Why not share your new insights with a friend?

Day Three   Continue practicing letters and words from this week's Scripture.

It.

Thessalonians

patience

into

Day Four   Write this week's Scripture verse on a sheet of practice paper.

May the Lord bring you into an ever deeper understanding of the love of God and of the patience that comes from Christ.

II Thessalonians 3:5

FOR DISCUSSION

What have you learned about the love of God this year? Why not share your new insights with a friend?

176

Scripture Verse

"Don't criticize and speak evil about each other, dear brothers. If you do, you will be fighting against God's law of loving one another."
James 4:11

Tip of the Week

Always look for the good in each other. Trade papers with a classmate, then point out each other's best letters and words.

Letter Focus

A a, D d, Z z

NOTE:
Directions must be used as part of the Weekly Lesson Format. See page 6.

TIP OF THE WEEK
Always look for the good in each other. Trade papers with a classmate, then point out each other's best letters and words.

Day One Practice the following letters and words from this week's Scripture.

A a

about

against

law

Day Two Continue practicing letters and words from this week's Scripture.

D d

do

dear

another

177

✏ Extended Teaching

• Coach students on specific things to look for as they exchange papers this week. Focus on spacing and alignment, or use all five goals of the **Five Star** evaluation.

• The contraction don't is found in this verse. Encourage students to practice writing two word combinations and their contractions (do not = don't; cannot = can't; would not = wouldn't; etc.)

✏ For Discussion

Compare this verse with Ephesians 4:2 (see lesson 23). How are they different? How are they similar?

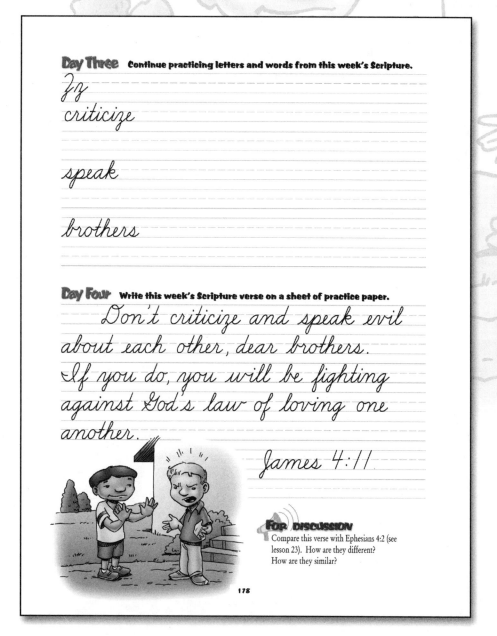

Day Three   Continue practicing letters and words from this week's Scripture.

Zz

criticize

speak

brothers

Day Four   Write this week's Scripture verse on a sheet of practice paper.

Don't criticize and speak evil about each other, dear brothers. If you do, you will be fighting against God's law of loving one another.

James 4:11

FOR DISCUSSION
Compare this verse with Ephesians 4:2 (see lesson 23). How are they different? How are they similar?

178

Please
Read This
First!

This appendix contains charts, lists, suggested activities, and other tools to enhance the *A Reason For*® **Handwriting** cursive workbooks.

Please note: Except for the Black Line Masters section (see page 165), all material in this Teacher Guidebook is copyright protected and may not be photocopied or duplicated in any form.

Appendix

Vocabulary List

This list is composed of all the practice words from the Transition Student Workbook.

Aa
abilities
about
against
all*
allowance
always
*and**
angels
another
anyone*
anything
answers
are*
as*
ask
asks
at*
away

Bb
back*
be*
beautiful
because
began
before
believes
belong
best
bless
blessed
blessings*
bring*
brothers

Cc
came
can
care
charm
child
children
Christ
Christian
church
citizens
Colossians
come
comes
coming
condemn
continue

country
created
criticize*
cross

Dd
day
dear
deep
deeper
didn't
different
disciples
do*
doing
done
don't*
down
dwell

Ee
each*
ears
earth
else
end
even
ever
everything*
evil
example
exception
exists
exit

Ff
face
family
Father*
faults
fellowship
filled
fine
first
follow
followers
for
forever
forgave
forgive
forgiven
forgiving

free
friendly
friends
*from**

Gg
Galatians
gentle
gentleness
get
give
given
glad
glory
go
God*
God's
good
grace
great
greatness
grow
grudges

Hh
harmony
has
have
he
hear
heart*
hearts
heaven
heavenly
help
helping
high
Him*
his
hold
holy*
home*
household
how*
humble

Ii
if
imitates
important
in
inside
instead
into*
is

Jj
James
Jesus
John

joy
just

Kk
kind
know

Ll
lasting
late
law
let*
life
light*
listen
listening
live
living
Lord*
love
loved
loving

Mm
make*
makes
making
many
Mark
marvelous
Matthew
may
measure
members
mind*
minds
mine
more
most
much*
must*
my

Nn
neighbor
never*
nothing

Oo
obey
of
oh
on
one*
other*
others*

Pp
patience
patient

peace*
people
perfect
personal
Peter
Phillipians
power
practice
praise*
pray
prayers
precious
prepare
prepared
presence*
prove
pure

Qq
quickly
quiet
quit

Rr
radiant
ready*
redeemed
rejoice
remain
remember
repay
repents
roots

Ss
satisfaction
Savior
says
Scriptures
set
should
show
size
snap
so
soil
some
Son
speak
special
spirit
strength
strong
sure*
sympathy

Tt
take
tell
tender

tenderhearted
terms
thank
that
the*
their
them
then*
there
Thessalonians
things
think
those*
time
to*
tomorrow
too
toward
true
trust
truth

Uu
understand
understanding
unkind
unless
use

Vv
visit

Ww
want*
wants*
watching
we*
well
what*
when
which
who*
whole
wide
will*
with*
within*
wonderful*
word
words
work
world
worry
worship
written

Yy
you*
your*
yourself

Skills List Index

Skills/letters emphasized in the Transition Workbook are found in the following lessons.

PRACTICE LETTERS

A
Capital: 9*, *1, 19, 24*, **2, 9, 16, 21, 27**
Lowercase: 2*, *1, 19, 24*, **2, 9, 16, 21**

B
Capital: 8*, *5, 15, 23*, **4, 5, 11, 13, 19**
Lowercase: 3*, *5, 15, 23*, **3, 4, 6, 8, 13, 19**

C
Capital: 8*, *4, 14*, **6, 11, 21, 24**
Lowercase: 2*, *4, 14*, **6, 16, 21, 24**

D
Capital: 8*, *1, 24*, **1, 16, 20, 27**
Lowercase: 2*, *1, 8, 24*, **1, 3, 4, 16, 20, 27**

E
Capital: 10*, *4, 17, 19, 26*, **2, 11, 20**
Lowercase: 2*, *4, 17, 26*, **2, 4, 11, 20**

F
Capital: 10*, *8, 19, 27*, **5, 8, 12, 15, 20**
Lowercase: 4*, *8, 27*, **3, 4, 8, 15, 20**

G
Capital: 8*, *2, 20, 25*, **5, 13, 19, 26**
Lowercase: 7*, *2, 20, 25*, **5, 13, 16, 19, 26**

H
Capital: 10*, *8, 17, 19, 22*, **6, 12, 17**
Lowercase: 3*, *8, 22*, **3, 4, 6, 12, 17, 19**

I
Capital: 10*, *9, 19, 21*, **5, 7, 15, 22**
Lowercase: 4*, *9, 21*, **7, 15, 22, 26**

J
Capital: 10*, *9*, **2, 15, 22**
Lowercase: 4*, 7*, *9*, **2, 7, 9, 15, 22**

K
Capital: 9*, *12*, **7, 12, 19, 23**
Lowercase: 3*, 4*, *12*, **3, 4, 7, 19, 23**

L
Capital: 10*, *6, 17, 19*, **4, 9, 12, 21**
Lowercase: 3*, *6, 8, 19*, **3, 4, 12, 21**

M
Capital: 9*, *7, 27*, **8, 10, 21, 25**
Lowercase: 6*, *7, 27*, **10, 18, 21, 25**

N
Capital: 9*, *7, 10*, **18**
Lowercase: 6*, *7, 10*, **18**

O
Capital: 8*, *2, 15*, **1, 10, 14, 25**
Lowercase: 2*, *2, 15*, **1, 8, 10, 14, 25**

P
Capital: 8*, *5, 17*, **4, 11, 18**
Lowercase: 7*, *5, 17*, **4, 11, 18**

Q
Capital: 8*, *3, 25*, **13, 22**
Lowercase: 7*, *3, 25*, **13, 16, 22**

R
Capital: 8*, *11, 23*, **3, 9, 11, 16, 26**
Lowercase: 6*, *11, 23*, **3, 9, 16, 26**

S
Capital: 10*, *13, 16*, **5, 11, 17**
Lowercase: 6*, *13, 16*, **5, 11, 17**

T
Capital: 10*, *13, 20, 26*, **3, 5, 7, 12, 26**
Lowercase: 3*, 4*, *8, 13, 20, 26*, **3, 4, 7, 12, 26**

U
Capital: 10*, *3, 10*, **3, 14, 23**
Lowercase: 6*, *3, 10*, **3, 13, 14, 18, 23**

V
Capital: 9*, *6, 18*, **5, 8, 17**
Lowercase: 5*, *6, 18*, **5, 8, 10, 17**

W
Capital: 9*, *11, 16*, **6, 18, 25**
Lowercase: 5*, *11, 16*, **6, 8, 18, 25**

X
Capital: 9*, *12, 18*, **8, 21, 23**
Lowercase: 5*, *12, 18*, **7, 8, 10, 21, 23, 12**

Y
Capital: 9*, *10, 22*, **1, 14, 21, 24**
Lowercase: 5*, 7*, *10, 22*, **1, 10, 14, 21, 24**

Z
Capital: 9*, *14, 21*, **21, 24, 27**
Lowercase: 5*, *14, 21*, **10, 21, 24, 27**

KEY:
* = Practice lessons (pages 9 - 18, Student Workbook)
Italics = Manuscript lessons (pages 21 - 74, Student Workbook)
Bold = Cursive lessons (pages 125 - 178, Student Workbook)

GENERAL SKILLS

IN EVERY VERSE
Letter formation
Number formation
Sentence structure
Punctuation
Capitalization

LETTER PRACTICE

Capital Letters
Boatstroke: **5**
Canestroke: **4, 14, 17, 19**
Circle: 8*, *25*
Curve: 10*
Downstroke: 10*, *7, 8, 9, 17, 23, 27*, **9, 21**
Forward curve: 8*, *23*
Forward oval: **11**
Oval: *2*, **11**
Slantstroke: 9*, *7, 10, 11, 18, 19, 27*
Tail: **1, 2, 14, 15**
Two stroke: 8*, *10, 13, 23, 28*, **7, 12, 19**
Three stroke: *8, 19*
Upswing: **22**

Lowercase Letters
Bridgestroke: **8, 18**
Circle: 2*, *2, 4, 5, 15, 24*
Curve: 6*, *7, 11, 22, 23*
Downstroke: 5*, *5, 8, 9, 11, 15*
Loop: **4, 19**
Oval: **16, 21**
Overstroke: **10**
Slantstroke: 5*, *6, 11, 18*
Tail: 7*, *25*, **29, 8, 13, 22**
Tall: 3*, *5, 6, 8, 15, 23*, **3, 6, 19**

Two stroke: 4*, *8, 9, 10, 11, 12, 13, 18, 27*, **7, 15, 26**
Upstroke: **9**

FIVE STAR SKILLS
Alignment: *3, 6, 26*, **9, 27**
Letter shape: *2, 5, 10, 14, 25*, **8, 16, 22**
Letter size: *4, 8, 14, 21, 29*, **3, 16, 22, 25, 30**
Letter slant: *6, 15, 26*, **11, 22, 28**
Letter spacing: *1, 17, 28*, **10, 17, 27**

MECHANICS
Paper position: *10, 24*, **23**
Pencil position: *12, 20*, **6, 12**
Posture: *10, 11, 24, 26*, **23**

OTHER PRACTICE
Evaluation: *1, 21, 30*, **1, 20, 27, 32**
Cap/lowercase review: 1*
Connected capitals: **2, 7, 17, 19, 29**
Connecting stroke: **13, 28**
Loop/Non-loop: **2, 4, 5, 17**
Manuscript review: **14**
Name focus: *3, 19*, **14, 30**
Number review: *14*
Similar cap/lowercase: *13, 16*, **14, 18, 21**
Verbal Description: 4*, *5, 7, 15, 19, 22, 29*
Visualize letter formation: 6*, 10*, *5, 17, 18, 22*

Letter Formation Charts

Cursive Letter Formation

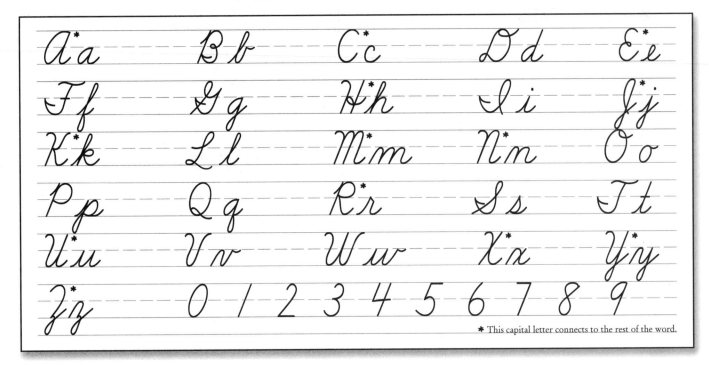

* This capital letter connects to the rest of the word.

Manuscript Letter Formation

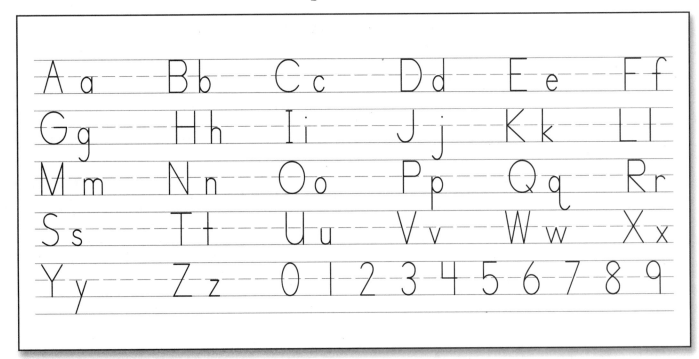

This information is also available in "Student Alphabet Desk Cards" or "Alphabet Wall Sheets." See your *A Reason For® Handwriting* catalog, or call (800) 447-4332.

Extended Activities

As students become more proficient at writing, these activites can be used to expand their opportunities for enjoyable and challenging practice.

Class Name Book
Write the name of each student on a 3 x 5 index card. Punch holes in these cards, then put them on a ring. This "Class Name Book" can be kept in the library or a favorite reading corner. Students will eagerly look for their own names, of course, but will soon begin recognizing other students' names as well.

The Writing Center
Develop a writing center where students can create "special messages." This activity offers yet another creative outlet for students to continually improve their handwriting. Special messages might include:

- Letters to family members
- Special occasion cards
- Thank-you notes
- Pen-pal messages
- Birthday cards
- Greeting cards
- Invitations
- Posters
- Letters to friends

Encourage students to come up with even more ideas for this activity. You can stock the writing center with items like:

- construction paper
- wallpaper sample books
- yarn or ribbons
- glue
- wrapping paper remnants
- old greeting cards
- scissors
- felt-tip pens
- tape

Include suggested messages, inspirational poems, and additional Scripture verses that students can incorporate into their creations.

Integrated Curriculum
Tie handwriting class into other core curricula. Every student workbook in *A Reason For*® **Handwriting** has a corresponding vocabulary list (page 150) which can be used as a basis for further practice. Ask students to write a sentence using each word from the list. The words may also be used as bonus spelling words or as the basis for a spelling bee.

Other Suggestions
It's amazing how creative students can be when given the chance! Brainstorm with your class about other extended activities they might enjoy. We'd love to hear what you come up with. (And maybe we'll even include your idea in a future edition of this Teacher Guidebook!)

Here's our address:

Carol Ann Retzer & Eva Hoshino
c/o Concerned Communications
P.O. Box 1000
Siloam Springs, AR 72761

Alternate Forms of
Handwriting Practice

Sky Writing

Sky Writing is a helpful way to practice the formation of individual letters. Demonstrate the letter formation with your pointer finger by "writing" in the air. Describe the letter as you demonstrate. For example, when making the capital A say, "Down, down, across." For the lowercase b say, "Down, up, around."

The class should then practice together. Go over the letter several times, with students and teacher Sky Writing together. After practicing, ask students to close their eyes and make the stroke(s) of the letter from memory.

When students open their eyes, have them "write" the letter on the palm of their left hand with the pointer finger of their right hand (reverse if the student is left-handed). Practice this several times, with students repeating the stroke descriptions aloud.

Back Writing

Students really enjoy this simple game! After you have introduced three or four new letters, choose one student to come to the front of the room to help you demonstrate.

Ask the student to stand with his or her back turned toward the class. Then use your pointer finger to "write" the letter on the student's back. Use big, definite strokes. Then, have the student guess which letter was outlined.

Once students understand the concept, you can have them work in pairs, taking turns "writing" and guessing letters.

Detailed Descriptions of Manuscript Letters

The lowercase a starts at the 2 o'clock position, goes up/around in a circle, then up to the ceiling and straight down to the floor. Don't lift your pencil, and make sure the circle touches the ceiling and floor.

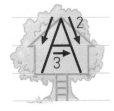

The capital A has three strokes. The first stroke starts at the roofline and slants down left to the floor. Return to the starting point and slant down right to the floor. The third stroke connects the first two at the ceiling.

The A stands for the ark and the animals in it. Read the story in your favorite Bible story book, then draw an ark and some animals. There should be seven of some animals, and two of others. Make sure to leave room for all of them in your picture!

The lowercase c begins at the 2 o'clock position, and circles up/around. It ends at the 4 o'clock position. Be sure the circle touches the ceiling and floor.

The capital C is made exactly like the lowercase c — only bigger! Make sure it touches the roofline at the top and the floor at the bottom.

The c begins a word we use a lot: come. "Come here." "Come help me!" Do you know how to ask someone to come without saying a word, just by using your hands? See how many people you can "talk" to without saying a word.

The lowercase b starts at the roofline and goes straight down to the floor, then circles up/around right, touching the ceiling and the floor. Don't lift your pencil.

The capital B has two strokes. Start at the roofline and go straight down to the floor. Lift your pencil. Return to the starting point and go around/down to the ceiling, then around/down to the floor.

B begins a very special word: Bible. Write it several times. Notice that this word has both a capital and a lowercase b in it. Just for fun, count how many Bibles there are in your classroom.

The lowercase d is like an a except the stick goes straight up to the roofline, then back down to the floor. Don't lift your pencil, and make sure the circle touches the ceiling and floor.

The capital D has two strokes. Start at the roofline and go straight down to the floor. Back at the starting point, go out/around and back down to the floor.

The word dove starts with d. Draw a dove. Keep your eyes open wide today, and maybe you can find a real feather to glue on your drawing!

Manuscript Letters
Continued

 The lowercase e starts with a straight line in the middle of the meeting room (left to right), then circles up/around and ends at the 4 o'clock position. Don't lift your pencil, and make sure the circle touches the ceiling and floor.

 The capital E has three strokes. Start at the roofline, go straight down to the floor, then straight right. Return to the starting point and make two short strokes to the right — one at the roofline, one at the ceiling.

Just for fun, write a lot of e's on a page, then add faces and hair to each one. Do your e's look like a bunch of people talking to each other?

 The lowercase g starts at the 2 o'clock position, goes up/around in a circle, then up to the ceiling and down to the ground with a monkey tail to the left. Don't lift your pencil. Make sure the circle touches the ceiling and floor.

 The capital G is made just like a capital C, but continue the circle up to the ceiling, then go straight to the left. Don't lift your pencil.

The word go begins with a g. Can you spell it? Write the word several times. Then draw a traffic signal showing a green light.

 The lowercase f starts in the attic with a canestroke. Circle up/around, then straight down to the floor. Lift your pencil and make a cross at the ceiling.

 The capital F is like an E without the bottom stroke. Start at the roofline and go straight down to the floor. Return to the starting point and make two short strokes to the right — one at the roofline, and a shorter one at the ceiling.

The word fruit begins with f. Name some different kinds of fruit you like. Draw a basket. Fill it with different kinds of fruit.

 The lowercase h starts at the roofline and goes straight down to the floor, then back up to the ceiling, circle over, and back down to the floor.

 The capital H has three strokes. The first stroke starts at the roofline and goes staight down to the floor. Make the second stroke parallel to the first. The third stroke connects the first two at the ceiling.

The word heart begins with an h. Draw several hearts in many sizes and colors. Start with a big heart, then draw smaller and smaller ones inside.

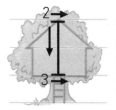

The lowercase i starts at the ceiling and goes straight down to the floor. Lift your pencil, then place the dot in the middle of the attic.

The capital I has three strokes. It begins at the roofline and goes straight down to the floor. Finish with a short line from left to right across the top, then across the bottom.

The ibex is a wild goat. Have someone help you find out where the ibex lives and what kind of horns it has. Try looking for it in the dictionary or an encyclopedia. God created lots of unusual animals for us to enjoy!

The lowercase k starts with a stroke from the roofline straight down to the floor. Lift your pencil. Now start at the ceiling and slant left/slant right and end at the floor.

The capital K begins with a stroke from the roofline to the floor. The second stroke starts at the roofline, slants left to touch the first line at the ceiling, then slants right down to the floor.

K is for the Kingdom where we all want to live someday. Revelation 21:16 - 21 describes it. Can you imagine how beautiful it will be? Draw a picture that shows some of the gold and the precious jewels that are there.

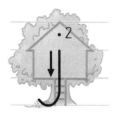

The lowercase j begins at the ceiling and goes straight down the ladder to the ground with a monkey tail to the left. Lift your pencil and place the dot in the middle of the attic.

The capital J begins at the roofline and goes straight down to the middle of the meeting room, curves left touching the floor, then curves back up to the middle of the meeting room.

The word jump starts with j. Can you jump for joy? See how many times you can jump rope without missing or stopping.

The lowercase l is one of the easiest letters! Begin at the roofline and go straight down to the floor. That's it!

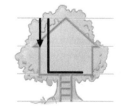

The capital L starts at the roofline and goes down to the floor. Turn right when you reach the floor to make a leg for it to stand on. Don't pick up your pencil.

The word light begins with an l. The Scriptures talk about our being lights that cannot be hidden. What are some ways that people can be lights? (Discuss this with students.) Now draw a picture of some kind of light.

Manuscript Letters
Continued

 The lowercase m begins at the ceiling, and goes straight down to the floor, then circles up/around/down, up/around/down. Make sure your humps touch the ceiling, and don't lift your pencil.

 The capital M starts with a stroke from the roofline straight down to the floor. Return to the starting point, then angle down to the floor, angle up to roofline, then straight down to the floor.

The word Mom begins with an M. Draw a picture for your mom to thank her for something she's done for you this week.

 The lowercase o starts at the 2 o'clock position and circles up/around and back to the start. Be sure it touches the ceiling and the floor.

 The capital O is exactly like the lowercase o, only bigger! It circles up/around and back to the start. Be sure it touches the roofline and the floor.

Open your eyes wide. Do they remind you of o's? Draw your eyes. (You may need to look in a mirror to see what color they are.) Now design a pair of glasses that you might like to wear.

 The lowercase n begins with a stroke from the ceiling straight down to the floor, then up/around/down, and back to the floor. Don't lift your pencil.

 The capital N starts with a stroke from the roofline straight down to the floor. Return to the starting point and angle down to the floor, then straight up to the roofline.

The word nice begins with an n. Why not try to be especially nice today? Do something helpful for someone — but don't tell anyone you did it!

 The lowercase p starts with a stroke from the ceiling straight down to the ground, then back up and circle around. Don't lift your pencil until you're finished.

 The capital P begins with a stroke from the roofline to the floor. Return to the starting point and circle around and down to the ceiling.

The word pet begins with a p. Draw a picture of your pet, or an animal you would like to have for a pet. If your pet is wild, be sure you draw a cage, too!

The lowercase q starts at the 2 o'clock position, goes up/around in a circle, then up to the ceiling and down to the ground with a monkey tail to the right. Don't lift your pencil. Make sure the circle touches the ceiling and floor.

The capital Q is made exactly like a capital O, but you add a short slanting line in the bottom right corner. Be sure the circle touches the roofline and the floor.

The title Queen begins with the letter Q. Find the story of brave Queen Esther in Scripture. Imagine how beautiful Esther's crown must have been. Draw a crown fit for a queen.

The lowercase letter s is a double curve letter. It begins at the 2 o'clock position, curves up to the left, then curves to the right in the middle of the meeting room, then back to the left, stopping at the 8 o'clock position.

The capital S is just like the lowercase s, only larger! Be sure it touches the roofline and the floor!

The word song begins with an s. Sometime today, sing a special song to someone who is really special!

The lowercase r begins with a stroke from the ceiling to the floor, then back up and over to the 2 o'clock position.

The capital R begins with a stroke from the roofline to the floor. Return to the starting point, and curve around and down to the ceiling, then angle right down to the floor.

The word rainbow begins with an r. See if you can find a Scripture story that talks about a rainbow. Draw a rainbow. Make sure your colors are in the right order. (Primary rainbow colors, from inside to outside, are violet, blue, green, yellow, orange, and red.)

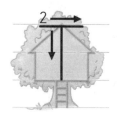

The lowercase t starts with a stroke from the roofline straight down to the floor. Lift your pencil, and then make a cross at the ceiling from left to right.

The capital T starts with a stroke from the roofline straight down to the floor. Lift your pencil, then make a cross at the roofline from left to right.

The word thankful begins with t. There are so many things that we can be thankful for! Draw a picture of at least three things that you are thankful for.

Manuscript Letters
Continued

The lowercase u begins at the ceiling. Go straight down toward the floor, curve around and back up to the ceiling, then straight down to end at the floor.

The capital U is just like the lowercase u, only bigger! Start at the roofline and go straight down toward the floor, curve around and back up to the roof, then straight down to end at the floor.

The word umbrella begins with u. Draw a picture of yourself under an umbrella. Are you staying dry? Then you should be smiling!

The lowercase w is made with one long stroke. Starting at the ceiling, slant down right to the floor, slant up to the ceiling, slant down to the floor, and slant up to the ceiling.

The capital W is just like the lowercase w, only bigger! Start at the roofline and slant down/slant up/slant down/slant up. Don't lift your pencil!

The word worm begins with w. Find out why worms are useful to gardeners. Make a "worm" by wrapping a pipe-cleaner around a pencil, then carefully pulling the pencil free. Tie a string to it, and you have a pet to pull around!

The lowercase v stays inside the meeting room. It starts at the ceiling and slants down right to the floor, then slants up right to the ceiling. Make sure you don't lift your pencil!

The capital V is just like the lowercase v, only bigger! The stroke is just the same except it starts and ends at the roofline: slant down/slant up. Make sure you don't lift your pencil.

The word vine begins with v. Jesus talks about the vine in one of His parables. Design a vine, making it cover as much of the page as you can. If you wish, you can draw a few birds or bugs hiding in the vine, too!

Both strokes in the lowercase x start at the ceiling and end at the floor. The first stroke slants down from left to right. The second slants down from right to left.

The capital X is just like the lowercase x, only bigger! Make sure that both strokes go from the roofline to the floor, and cross at the ceiling.

Not many words *begin* with x, but the word exit has an x as the second letter. Draw an exit sign that you could put by the door leading out of the classroom or your room at home.

The first stroke of the y slants right from the ceiling down to the floor. The second slants left from the ceiling down to the ground — touching the first at the floor.

Begin the capital Y by making a lowercase v in the attic. Make sure it touches the roofline and the ceiling. The second stroke goes from the bottom of the v straight down to the ground.

A y word that we use often is yes. Practice writing this word, then talk about questions that should have "yes" answers.

The lowercase z is a one-stroke letter starting at ceiling. Make a line straight right, slant left down to the floor, then make a line straight right.

The capital Z is just like the lowercase z, only bigger! Use the same zigzag stroke — straight right/slant down/straight right. Remember it must touch the roofline and the floor.

The word zoo begins with a z. Draw a picture of a zoo animal that begins with the letter z. Here's a hint: It's an animal looks like a horse with stripes! (Zebra)

Letter Groups

Children often enjoy discovering the similarities and differences between letters — much like sorting buttons by size, color, or shape. This activity helps children form clear mental models of letters and strokes, leading to more accurate letter formation and better handwriting.

As you explore the following groups with your students, be sure to remind them that some letters have multiple characteristics, and so can be included in more than one group. (A good example is the lowercase b.)

CAPITAL GROUPS
Circle (C, G, O, Q)
Curve (J, S, U)
Downstroke (B, D, E, F, H, I, J, K, L, M, N, P, R, T, U)
Forward curve (B, D, P, R)
Single stroke (C, G, J, L, O, S, U, V, W, Z)
Slantstroke (A, K, M, N, V, W, X, Y, Z)
Two-stroke (B, D, K, M, N, P, Q, R, T, X)
Three-stroke (A, E, F, H, I)

LOWERCASE GROUPS
Circle (a, b, c, d, e, g, o, p, q)
Curve (h, m, n, r, s, u)
Downstroke (b, f, h, i, j, k, l, m, n, p, r, t)
Slantstroke (k, v, w, x, y, z)
Tail (g, j, p, q, y)
Tall (b, d, f, h, k, l, t)
Two-stroke (f, i, j, k, t, x, y)

Cursive Letter Groups

Many letters in cursive writing use similar patterns in their formation. **Letter Group Charts** help focus attention on these similarities, enhancing the understanding of letter formation. These groupings are also helpful for introducing new letters, and for providing direction in continued practice. (Please note that most letters have features that apply to more than one group.)

The following descriptions help identify similar characteristics of LOWERCASE cursive letters:

Oval letters

a c d g o p q

Upstroke letters

i j p r s t u w

Loop letters

b e f h k l

Tail letters

f g j p q y z

Tall letters

b d f h k l t

Overstroke letters

m n v x y z

Bridgestroke letters

b o v w

Two-Stroke letters

i j t x

The following descriptions help identify similar characteristics of CAPITAL cursive letters:

Oval capitals

A C E O

Foward Oval capitals

B P R

Boatstroke capitals

B F G I S T

Canestroke capitals

H K M N U V W X Y

Upswing capitals

I J Q

Tail capitals

J Y Z

Downstroke capitals

L D

Two- and Three-stroke capitals

F H K T X

Please Read This First!

PLEASE PHOTOCOPY!*

The following pages contain Black Line Masters for use with the *A Reason For®* Handwriting workbooks. Please feel free to photocopy these pages for use in your classroom.* Here are some suggested uses:

Getting Ready To Write! (page 167) makes a great mini-poster.

The Treehouse (page 169) can easily be made into an overhead transparency. A detailed description of how to use the treehouse can be found in the Manuscript A or Manuscript B Teacher Guidebooks.

Five Star Evaluation Examples (page 171 and 173) can be made into an overhead transparency, or copied for individual handouts. This page helps illustrate various points of the *Five Star* grading system (see page 9).

The **Handwriting Evaluation Form** (page 175) is a multiple master. Copy, then cut each page into four individual forms. For a detailed description of how to use this form in grading, see page 9.

Manuscript Handwriting
Getting Ready To Write!

1. Be Comfortable. Clear other books and papers off your desk. Sit well back in the chair with your feet flat on the floor. Your eyes should not be too close to the paper—10 to 15 inches is ideal.

2. Hold your pencil correctly (about 1/2″ above the sharpened part).

3. Keep your wrist straight, allowing your arm to move freely.

4. Place your writing paper at an angle. (It should be in line with your writing arm.)

5. Work to make your letters the right size. Remember that all small letters should come to the middle dotted line. Capitals should all be the same size—from the top line to the bottom line.

6. Have a good attitude. Be positive about handwriting.

7. Take enough time to write neatly. Your handwriting makes a statement about you!

8. Practice doing your very best.

The Treehouse

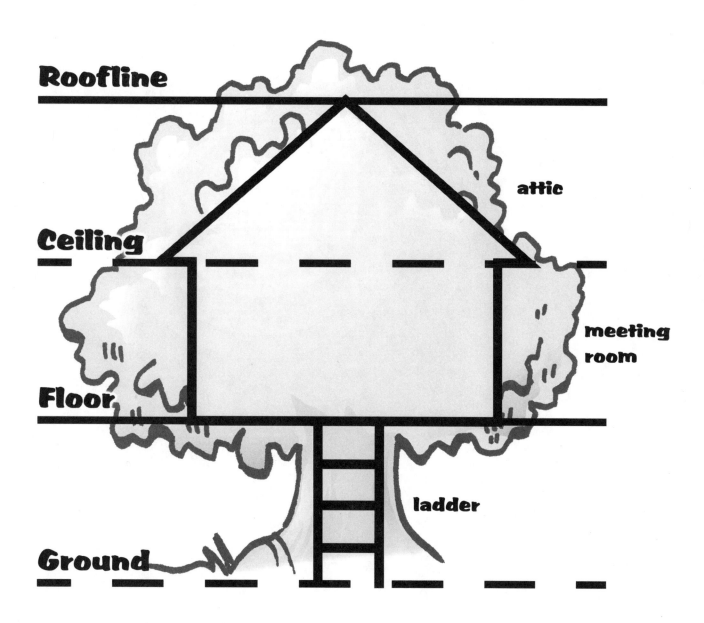

Roofline

attic

Ceiling

meeting room

Floor

ladder

Ground

Five Star
Manuscript Examples

Example 1
Allignment

Improved Form

helper   helper

Example 2
Slant

Improved Form

half day   half day

Example 3
Size

Improved Form

blesses   blesses

Example 4
Shape

Improved Form

succeed   succeed

Example 5
Spacing

Improved Form

was joyful   was joyful

Five Star
Cursive Examples

Example 1
Alignment   Improved Form

willing helper   *willing helper*

Example 2
Slant   Improved Form

half a day   *half a day*

Example 3
Size   Improved Form

blesses   *blesses*

Example 4
Shape   Improved Form

succeed   *succeed*

Example 5
Spacing   Improved Form

was joyful   *was joyful*

 **Handwriting Evaluation Form**

● Two points possible for each ●

Alignment
Letters/words sit on the line _____

Slant
Letters have the same slant _____

Size
Capital & lowercase letters
are the correct size _____

Shape
Letters are shaped correctly
and neatly _____

Spacing
Letters and words are
spaced correctly _____

TOTAL _____

 **Handwriting Evaluation Form**

● Two points possible for each ●

Alignment
Letters/words sit on the line _____

Slant
Letters have the same slant _____

Size
Capital & lowercase letters
are the correct size _____

Shape
Letters are shaped correctly
and neatly _____

Spacing
Letters and words are
spaced correctly _____

TOTAL _____

 **Handwriting Evaluation Form**

● Two points possible for each ●

Alignment
Letters/words sit on the line _____

Slant
Letters have the same slant _____

Size
Capital & lowercase letters
are the correct size _____

Shape
Letters are shaped correctly
and neatly _____

Spacing
Letters and words are
spaced correctly _____

TOTAL _____

 **Handwriting Evaluation Form**

● Two points possible for each ●

Alignment
Letters/words sit on the line _____

Slant
Letters have the same slant _____

Size
Capital & lowercase letters
are the correct size _____

Shape
Letters are shaped correctly
and neatly _____

Spacing
Letters and words are
spaced correctly _____

TOTAL _____